Anonymus

The Liquefaction Of The Blood Of St. Januarius, At Naples

An Historical And Critical Examination Of The Miracle

Anonymus

The Liquefaction Of The Blood Of St. Januarius, At Naples
An Historical And Critical Examination Of The Miracle

ISBN/EAN: 9783743348158

Manufactured in Europe, USA, Canada, Australia, Japa

Cover: Foto ©Lupo / pixelio.de

Manufactured and distributed by brebook publishing software
(www.brebook.com)

Anonymus

The Liquefaction Of The Blood Of St. Januarius, At Naples

RELIQUARY CONTAINING THE VIALS OF THE BLOOD OF ST. JANUARIUS AT NAPLES. *pp.* 3, 4.

SCALE—*Nearly one-half natural size.*

A, A, Dark and rough masses of soldering holding the vials in place.   B, B, Stains or pellicles of the blood on the interior of the smaller vial.

THE

LIQUEFACTION

OF THE

BLOOD OF ST. JANUARIUS,

AT NAPLES.

An Historical and Critical Examination of the Miracle.

NEW YORK:

THE CATHOLIC PUBLICATION SOCIETY,

No. 9 WARREN STREET.

1872.

On the nineteenth day of September, there will be gathered together from five to eight thousand persons in the grand cathedral of Naples, to witness again an occurrence which, though it has been witnessed thousands of times already, never fails to fill the beholder with astonishment and awe. Perhaps one-half of the crowd may be from the city of Naples itself. A large portion comes from other parts of Italy. Many are from Austria, Illyria, Hungary, Bavaria, and Prussia, Russia, England, France, and Spain. Some are from the Western hemisphere. And Moors, Egyptians, Arabs, and Turks, ever travelling along the shores of the Mediterranean, are here, too, raising their turbaned heads among these thousands in the cathedral, as intent and as filled with emotion as any around them.

The greater part of that crowd believe that they are witnesses of a deed done by the direct will and power of God—a miracle; and very naturally their hearts are filled with awe and devotion. Others, again, are in doubt what to believe on the point; but they have come to see, and to see exactly for themselves what really does occur. Others, again, are sure beforehand that it is all a trick. They will spare no pains to detect the fraud.

What is it they are all assembled to see? The large cathedral in which they stand fronts on a little square to the north. At the southern extremity is placed the grand sanctuary and high altar, with a large and rich basement chapel underneath. On either side of the church above,

there are, as is usual in Italian churches, small side chapels and altars; but about the middle of the western side a large archway gives admission to a very large chapel—to-day the centre of attraction. We might call it a small church. The Neapolitans name it the *Tesoro*. It is cruciform, and a well-proportioned dome rises above the intersection of its nave and transept. Towards its western extremity, and opposite the crowded archway or entrance from the cathedral, stands its elevated high altar; six other altars occupy the transept and sides. The main altar stands about five feet forward, out from the solid stone wall of the building. Behind that altar, in the massive masonry of the wall, is a double closet, closed by strong metal doors, and secured by four locks. From this closet, at nine A.M., is first taken out a metal life-sized bust, held to contain what remains of the bones of the head of St. Januarius, bishop and martyr, who was put to death in the year 305. This bust is placed on the main altar, at the Gospel end. Next, an old and tarnished silver case is brought out from the other side of the same closet. All eyes scrutinize it. The front and the back of it, or, rather, both faces of it, for they are alike, are of heavy glass, securely fastened to the silver frame. Looking through these plates of glass, the interior of the case is seen to contain two antique Roman vials of glass, held securely in their places above and below by rude masses of soldering, black with age. The vials are of different patterns, both very common in the museums of Roman antiquities. The smaller one is empty, save some patches of stain or pellicle adhering to the interior of its sides. The other one, which might hold a gill and a half, is seen to contain a dark-colored solid substance, occupying about four-fifths of the space within the vial. This substance is held to be a portion of the blood of the same martyred saint, gathered by the Christians when he was decapitated, and ever since carefully preserved. Ordinarily it is hard and solid, as it well may be fifteen hundred and sixty-odd years after being shed. The case, or *reliquary*, as it is properly called, is borne to the main altar, and a priest holds it midway between the middle of the altar and the bust, that is, about a foot from the latter. Prayers are said; hymns, psalms, and litanies are recited by the clergy kneeling near. Meanwhile, from time to time the priest moves the reliquary from side to side, that he may see whether the expected change of the substance within the vial has taken place or not; and he presents it to the bystanders crowded around him on the steps of the altar, that each one in succession may reverently kiss it and closely scrutinize its condition. At length, after a greater or smaller lapse of time, perhaps in a few minutes, perhaps only after several hours, perhaps after many hours, the solid mass within the vial becomes liquid—perhaps instantaneously, perhaps rapidly, at times more slowly and gradually, several hours elapsing before the change becomes complete. Sometimes only a portion of the mass becomes liquid, the remaining portion floating as a still hard lump in the liquid portion. This change is what is known as *the liquefaction of the blood of St. Januarius*, and is what these thousands have crowded the

Tesoro chapel and the cathedral to witness.

It has occurred repeatedly each year for centuries back. It occurs in public under the eyes of thousands. Accounts of it were written by learned men and by travellers before the invention of printing. In these latter centuries, accounts of it have been published in Latin, in Italian, in Polish, in English, French, German, and Spanish—we presume, in every language of Europe. Some are written by devout believers in the miracle; some by candid but perplexed witnesses, who examined for themselves and are afraid to come to a conclusion; while others that we have seen are filled with such mistakes, both as to persons and events and to established regulations, that we felt the writers had themselves seen little or nothing. They had merely got a hint from one and a suggestion from another, and had filled out the remainder from the storehouse of their own imagination.

We are privileged to insert a full account, written by an American eye-witness in 1864. We are unwilling to abbreviate it too much, although the reader will find in it thoughts we have already expressed or may hereafter have to dwell on:

I had for years determined that, if ever I had a chance, I would go to Naples to see myself the celebrated miracle. This year gave me the desired opportunity, and I would not neglect it. Leaving Rome by railway, on September 17, I reached Naples that evening, and early the next morning went to the cathedral to introduce myself, to say Mass, and to take a preparatory look. The cathedral is an immense semi-Gothic building, dedicated to the Blessed Virgin, to St. Januarius, and to other patron saints of the city. St. Januarius, a native of Naples, was Bishop of Benevento (a city some thirty miles inland), and was apprehended in the days of persecution under Diocletian, held in prison, exposed to the wild beasts without harm, and finally beheaded near Puzzuoli, about five miles from Naples, in the year 305. His head and body were taken by the Christians, and transported—probably by night, certainly in secrecy—across the bay to the southern shore, and were entombed, between Mount Vesuvius and the sea, on the farm of a Christian called Marcian. It was the custom of the Christians to gather, as far as they possibly could, the blood shed by their martyrs, and, placing a portion of it in glass vials, to deposit such vials in the tombs. In the catacombs at Rome such vials in a niche are the surest sign that a martyr was there deposited. You can still see some of them, or fragments of them, in the opened vaults or niches of the catacombs. The vials within have a thin, dark-reddish crust, showing still where the blood reached in the glass. A few years ago, a chemical analysis of a portion of such crust or pellicle, made by direction of his Holiness, fully confirmed this historical and traditional statement of its origin. Such vials are also to be seen in multitudes in the Vatican and other Christian museums, and in the churches to which the remains of the martyrs have been transferred. As St. Januarius was a prominent Christian, and as his martyrdom attracted the earnest attention of all, we may and should naturally suppose that his case was no exception, and that a portion of the blood was gathered in his case, and, as usual, that the vials containing it were deposited with the body in the tomb.

In the year 385, peace having been fully restored, and Christian churches built, and things quieted, the remains of St. Januarius were solemnly transferred from their original resting-place to Naples, and were placed in a church or chapel dedicated to him, and situated just outside the city walls. *San Gennaro extra muros* still stands, though, of course, the first building has been replaced by a second, a third, I believe by a fourth church. Here, henceforth, near their martyr and patron saint, the Neapolitan Christians wished to be buried. And when an oath was to be taken with the most binding force and obligation, it was administered and taken before the altar where lay enshrined the remains of this great Neapolitan saint. In course of time—it is not precisely known when, or by what archbishop—the head of St. Januarius and

the *ampulla* or vials containing his blood were transferred into the city, and placed in some church—probably in the cathedral, where we know that, eight hundred years ago, they were carefully and reverently preserved in the cathedral, *Tesoro* or treasury, as they called the strong, vaulted chamber of stone in which the relics of the saints were safely kept. The body of the saint was left in the church *extra muros*. It was afterwards taken to Benevento, thence to Monte Vergine, and in 1497 was transferred to Naples, and now lies under the principal altar of the subterranean crypt or basement chapel, beneath the sanctuary of the cathedral.

The cathedral itself is, as I said, a large semi-Gothic building, over three hundred feet long and one hundred and twenty wide, lofty, well-proportioned, and filled with columns, frescoes, marbles, statuary, paintings, and gilding, very bright and very clean. It fronts on a small square to the north. The sanctuary is at the southern end. In the west side of the building is a large, open archway, about thirty feet broad and forty feet high, with a lofty open-work railing of bronzed metal, and of very artistic design. A folding-door in this railing, of the same material, opens twelve feet wide to usher you into another good-sized church or chapel, called the new *Tesoro* or chapel of St. Januarius, commenced in 1608, by the city, in special honor of the saint, and in fulfilment of a vow, and consecrated in 1646. It is nearly in the form of a Greek cross, over a hundred feet from east to west, and about eighty from north to south. The arms are about forty feet wide, and at their intersection a cupola rises to over a hundred feet above the level of the floor. It is said this chapel cost half a million of dollars If so, the city fathers got the full worth of their money in rich marbles, in mosaics, frescoes, bronze and marble statues, and in every sort of finest decorations. There is a complete service for this chapel, entirely distinct from and independent of that of the cathedral proper—a dean, twelve chaplains, other minor assistants as needed, and a thoroughly supplied sacristy. In this *Tesoro* chapel are no less than seven altars ; the main one, to the west, opposite the entrance from the church, another grand one, and two subsidiary ones on either side of the chapel. There is also a fine organ. The main altar stands about five feet forward from the rear wall of the building, leaving thus a commodious passage-way between them. In the massive stone wall itself, to the rear of the main altar, are two armories, adjoining each other. In one of them, that to the south, the relic of the head of St. Januarius is kept; in the other, to the north, are preserved the vials containing his blood. These armories, which I might call a double armory, are in the solid masonry, and are closed by strong gilt metal doors, about thirty inches broad and fifty inches high, each secured by an upper and a lower lock.

So much I saw at this visit in the cathedral and in the chapel. The afternoon I devoted to a visit to Puzzuoli, and the scene of the martyrdom of St. Januarius and his six companions. On the way, we stopped to look at and enter the reputed tomb of Virgil, and we passed through the grotto of Posilippo. As the carriage rolled on over the smooth macadamized road, the Bay of Naples stretched away on our left in all its beauty, smiling and rippling in the September breeze, just as it did on the day they were beheaded. Before us was Puzzuoli, once the beautiful summer resort and watering-place for the richest nobles of ancient Rome, often graced by the presence of the emperor himself, and still a place of pretension. On our right, hills and vineyards and olive groves stood now as they stood then. The palaces and houses which the saint looked on are all gone; but their solid stone foundation walls have not perished, and other houses of more modern aspect rise on them. The mineral springs at the foot of the hills are still the same, and in the same repute; and hundreds are still going to them, or meet us returning after their baths. Here and there, alongside our smooth modern road, we see patches of the old Roman pavement, large, irregularly-shaped slabs of hard stone, lying now much less evenly than they did when senators, and consuls, and prefects, and Roman nobles loved to walk along this road, to enjoy the beautiful scene, and to drink in the healthful evening breezes that came to them over the Mediterranean.

We reached Puzzuoli, and its narrow, crooked streets soon led us to the summit of a knoll or spur of the hills, now a little back of the modern city. Here

the ancients had placed their amphithe atre. Its remains are still well preserved. The galleries for the dignitaries, the seats for the spectators—it could hold 15,000 at least—the arena, where the gladiators fought and fell, and where wild beasts tore each other or destroyed their human victims, are all still to be easily recognized. We entered a cellar or masonry chamber under the lofty seats. Here the victims were kept until the hour came for thrusting them forth into the arena in the centre. It is now a chapel, with a single plain altar, at which Mass is celebrated from time to time. A votive lamp hangs down from the arched masonry above The walls are plain and void of ornament. The place needs little decoration. Who can kneel there, and not feel his heart swell as he remembers St. Januarius and his companions kneeling and praying, and awaiting their summons? It came, and they were led forth. We went, too, to the arena. Here they stood, sustained by the constancy of faith. There is the seat aloft of the prefect and his attendants and officers, who condemned these Christians to death by the wild beasts, and have come to look on the bloody drama. There, all around, rising backwards, row above row, are the seats, filled then by thousands hoarsely screaming, "*The Christians to the lions!*" To their voices answered the angry growls and roars of lions and panthers, shut in their dens beneath—those recesses in the masonry below the lowest, the front rank of seats. For one or two days past the beasts have been deprived of their food, that they might be more furious and eager for the tragedy. Excited by the clamor, maddened by hunger, frenzied, too, perhaps by the sight of the victims, whom they could see through the bars of their doors —for perhaps they had already had experience of such feasts—the beasts walked impatiently from end to end of their small prisons, glared and growled through the bars, or impatiently strove to tear them down. The prefect gives the signal: the multitude is hushed in silent expectation. The servitors hurry forward to the edge of the seats above, and with cords and pulleys are lifting upwards the heavy doors in their grooves. The iron grates against the stone as it mounts. Soon out from below into the arena leap the ravenous wild beasts. They rush on, each one intent on seizing a victim. They crouch, as is their nature, for a final spring, fastening their glaring eyes on the martyrs; but they spring not. The eye loses its glare; the stiffened mane and bristling hair become smooth, and, with moans almost of affection, they draw themselves gently over the sand up to the martyrs, and fawn on them and lick their feet. There will be no bloody tragedy here to-day. God vouchsafes to the prefect Timotheus and to these multitudes another proof of the saintly character and heavenly authority of these men whom they would slay. Some, we may hope, were awed, and believed, and returned to their homes with hearts yielding to the grace of God; but not so the prefect, nor the majority of that crowd. 'Sorcery! Witchcraft! Chaldean superstition!" they cried. "Away with the dangerous magicians! If they can do this, what can they not do? Who is safe? Slay them at once!" The prefect ordered them to be led out to the top of a neighboring hill, and to be beheaded on its summit in the sight of all and as a warning to all. We followed the steep and narrow old Roman road up which they must have walked. The rains have not yet washed away all of the old Roman pavement. Vines and olive-trees and flowers of richest hues shade it and beautify it now, and were not wanting to it in those days of imperial luxury. To our martyrs it was the road to heaven. No earthly beauty could cheer them as they were cheered by Christian faith and the firm hopes of quickly reaching a blessed immortality. We reached the spot of execution, the level top of a knoll, overlooking some part of the city, the beautiful bay, Puzzuoli, and much of the neighboring country. A little church stands here now, served by a small community of Capuchins, who hold the faith of the martyrs, and try to imitate their virtues; who seek first the kingdom of heaven and its righteousness, and hope that, like the martyrs they honor, they may pass from this consecrated spot to the abode of bliss. Here the saint and his six companions were beheaded. The Capuchins showed us in the church a stone, now inserted in the wall and carefully preserved, said to have been stained by his blood, and still to show the stains. They said, too, that, when the blood of St. Januarius liquefies in Naples, these stains grow moist and assume a brighter red-

dish color. This I had no opportunity of verifying. Here, too, we might almost guess the route down the precipitous sides of the hill to the waters of the bay, almost under our feet, by which that night the Christians bore the body of the saint to their boat. Across the bay, five or six miles off, we could see the houses of Torre dell' Annunziata, near where they landed with it. A little back lay the farm of the Christian where they entombed it. A Benedictine monastery from the sixth century marked the spot. . . .

As you may well suppose, night overtook us before we got back to Naples. The next morning, I went to the cathedral again. It was the 19th of September, the festival proper of the saint—the day of his martyrdom and entrance into heaven. The exposition of his relics, during which the liquefaction usually occurs, commences at nine A.M. I was at the door of the chapel at half-past eight. I found the chapel already crammed and jammed. Still, way was made for me somehow. I went to the sacristy, and was then conducted back to the chapel, and into the space behind the main altar, in front of the armories, to await the hour appointed. Of course, the crowd could not yet enter the sanctuary of the main altar, much less pass behind the altar. Only five or six privileged persons were there. Mass was being celebrated at the altar itself. That over, we sat and waited, and I asked questions on the all-absorbing subject.

Since the building and opening of this new *Tesoro* chapel — that is, since A.D. 1646—the relics are in the keeping of the Archbishop of Naples and the city authorities conjointly. Everything is regulated by the long and minute agreement then entered into by all parties. I said each door of the armories has two locks. The archbishop keeps the key of one, the city authorities the key of the other. The armories cannot be approached except through the open chapel, and cannot be opened, save by violence, unless both parties are present with their keys.

I was patiently waiting for nine o'clock to strike. Our number was increasing. At last there joined us behind the altar a tall, thin, gentlemanly man, all in black, about forty-five years of age. He was introduced to me as Count C——, the delegate to-day on the part of the city. He bore a large red velvet purse or bag with gold cords and braiding, very rich in its workmanship. Opening its mouth, he drew forth two good-sized, long-handled antique keys with complicated wards. They were connected by a steel chain, strong and light, about fifteen inches in length. The cardinal, Riario Sforza, is absent in Rome, driven into exile by Victor Emmanuel's government; but before leaving he gave his keys in charge to one of the chief ecclesiastics of the city in his stead. Accordingly, a canon of the cathedral soon appeared, bearing another red velvet bag, something like the first, but not so rich, and, moreover, somewhat faded. He, too, took out of his bag two good-sized, long-handled keys, equally antique in their look and complicated in their wards, and similarly connected by a steel chain. Count C—— inserted one of his keys in the lower lock of the armory to the south, and turned it. We heard the bolt shoot back. The pious-looking canon was short, and the upper lock was rather high, so they placed some portable steps in position. He ascended them, and inserted one of his keys in the upper lock. That bolt shot back, too ; and he swung the heavy metal door open. We looked into the interior of the armory, about two feet wide, three and a-half or four feet high, and sixteen or twenty inches deep, in the masonry of the wall. It was lined with slabs of white marble, and a scarlet silk curtain hung down towards the front. A thick metal partition divided it from the other armory. One of the chaplains of the *Tesoro* then mounted the steps, and took out from the armory a life-sized bust of St. Januarius, of silver gilt. A mitre on the head of it, and a short cope which had been put on the shoulders, designated his episcopal character. In the head of this bust are contained the relics of the head of the saint.

We know precisely when this bust was made; for in the spring of 1306 an entry was made in the account-books of Charles of Anjou, then sovereign of Naples, stating how much silver and how much gold from the king's treasury had been given to a certain artificer as materials, and how much money was paid to him for his workmanship, in making this very bust. In making it, he modelled the features after a very ancient bust of the saint, still existing in Puzzuoli. In the archiepiscopal diary, relative to St. Januarius, under the date 13th September-

ber, 1660, there is a long account stating that, it being perceived that the relics inside this bust had become somehow displaced—as well they might after 355 years—the cardinal archbishop, on that day, in the presence of all requisite witnesses, had the bust opened by a goldsmith ; himself reverently took out the relics, and held them in his hands until the goldsmith had repaired the damage ; that his eminence then reverently replaced the relics, properly sealed, and had the bust closed as before, and in all this carefully observed the prescriptions of canon law. Since then, everything has been untouched.

Four other chaplains, with torches, attended the chaplain whom I saw take out this bust, and it was borne in procession round to the front of the altar, and deposited on the altar itself, just where the missal would stand when the Gospel is read. They then returned to the armory.

Count C—— with his second key unlocked the lower lock of the other—the northern armory. The little canon again mounted the steps, unlocked the upper one, and swung back the metal door. We looked into the armory : it was just the fellow of the first—size, marble lining, red silk curtain, and all. The same chaplain then, as before, took out the reliquary containing the *ampulla* or vials of the blood. I will describe it. Conceive a bar or thick plate of silver, about two and a-half inches wide and about sixteen inches long, to be bent until it forms a ring or circle of about five inches diameter. Let a circular plate of glass of the requisite diameter be inserted and firmly fastened to the edge of the silver ring on one side, and a similar plate of glass be also inserted and firmly fastened to the other edge. You will thus have, as it were, the centre-piece of an ostensory, five inches across and two and one half inches through, with a silver rim, and glass plates forming the front and rear. On the top, let there be a little ornamental scroll-work, cherubs and their wings, and a central stem rising upward, and bearing an oval crown three inches by two inches, and above that a small elegantly-worked silver crucifix. Below the circular rim, attach a round, hollow bar of silver, about one inch in diameter and three inches long. It will serve as a stem to hold the reliquary by, or as a foot which may be inserted into an opening fitted to receive it. The reliquary may thus be kept upright, whether it be placed on a stand on the altar or put away in its armory. This reliquary is strong and plain, with very little ornamentation on the silver, but that, they say, in very good style. Inside this frame, or case, or reliquary, between the front and rear glass, and perfectly visible through them, stand two *ampullæ* or vials of glass, both fastened to the silver rim at top and at bottom by rough, irregular masses of dark soldering. They are held to be the identical glass vials in which a portion of the blood of St. Januarius was poured at the time of his martyrdom, which were laid in his tomb, and, in 385, were brought with his body to Naples, and which have ever since been carefully and reverently preserved. They are of the old Roman patterns and material. One may see hundreds of just such vials in the museums of Naples and Rome. One of them is long and narrow, like a modern vial, yet not so even and symmetrical. The neck, too, does not narrow in the manner of modern vials. A fillet runs three or four times round it just below the neck. Perhaps it was an ornament; more probably it was intended by the maker to prevent the little vial from slipping when held between the fingers. The other *ampulla* or vial is of a different pattern. Its height is the same; the neck is a little higher up, and is encircled by a single fillet of an undulating curvature. The lower portion swells out until it is two inches in diameter, and the vial would hold, I judge, about a gill and a-half. In the interior of the first *ampulla*, I saw two patches resembling the pellicle which I had seen, at Rome, left on the inner surface of the glass vases after the martyrs' blood originally contained in them had entirely evaporated or passed away. The other vial, THE AMPULLA, contains a substance ordinarily hard, dark, with a reddish or purple hue, and filling ordinarily three-fourths of the space within the vial, perhaps a little more. This substance is held to be a portion of the blood of St. Januarius, still retained in this vial, in which it was originally placed on September 19, A.D. 305.

In this description of the reliquary and the *ampullæ*, I have, of course, summed up the result of all the careful and scrutinizing observations which I had the opportunity of making. I have not been able to learn when this silver reliquary or case was made. No entry is found settling the point, as in the case of the bust. The style of ornamentation on the silver case and on the crown would indicate about the same epoch of art. But I am inclined to think it the earlier made of the two. Charles of Anjou showed himself to be too liberal in the matter of the bust to be suspected of being a niggard in preparing the reliquary, and those coming after him would have felt bound to be guided by the example of his liberality. It was probably made some time before the year 1300, possibly even by Roger, King of Sicily, who visited Naples about A.D. 1140.

But to go back. As the chaplain took the reliquary out from the armory, he examined it, and said, "*E duro e pieno*"—"*It is hard and full.*" In fact, the larger vial, as he showed the reliquary round to each one of the eight or ten persons behind the altar, and as I most clearly saw it, was filled to the very top, I could not be mistaken in that; but whether the contents were liquid or solid, I really could not tell. For the very fulness prevented any change being visible, at least to my eyes, in that uniformly dark mass, even if the contents were liquid, although the reliquary was moved freely from side to side, held horizontally, or even reversed. After we had each one venerated and fully examined the reliquary, the canon, with his attendants bearing torches, bore it in procession to the front of the altar, and showed it aloft to the people. I followed immediately behind, and ascended the steps of the altar with them. On the platform in front of the altar, we were four: 1. The chaplain, holding the reliquary in his hands by the stem I have spoken of. He stood facing the altar, or leaning over it, between the middle and the Gospel end, where now stood the bust. 2. In front of the bust, and close to the first chaplain, on his left, stood a second chaplain, bearing a lighted taper in a silver hand-candlestick. He would sometimes hold this in such a position, eight or ten inches off from the reliquary and behind it, that the light from it would shine on the interior, so that the observer would not be troubled by the reflection of the ordinary light from the surface of the plate of glass next to him. 3. Count C——, the city delegate, stood at the right of the first chaplain, and, therefore, in front of the middle of the altar. It is his sworn duty not to lose sight of the precious reliquary from the moment the doors of the armory are opened at nine A.M., until it is replaced there, and duly locked up, about half an hour after sunset. He cannot retire from his post at any time, unless his place is supplied by an alternate delegate, who has been chosen, and who, I was told, had promised to come by 11 A.M. 4. Next to Count C——, I stood, or rather knelt, until the people crowded so on me that I positively had not room to continue in that position.

The people, now that the Mass had been over for twenty minutes or so, had entered the sanctuary, or had been introduced into it. They completely filled the space within the rails; they stood crowded on the steps; they even invaded the platform itself, not a very large one, forcing the attendant chaplains, who had borne the torches in the procession, and who now remained to join with the two chaplains at the altar in the prayers, to retire somewhat, and kneel in a group, off at the end of the altar; forced the count and myself of necessity to stand; and just left a little room for the two chaplains to turn in, barely sufficient.

As I stood up. I could see the crowd. The chapel was filled; there are, you know, no pews or seats in Italian churches; all were standing as closely as possible together. The sanctuaries of the side chapels were equally crowded; men stood on the steps and platforms of their altars; the very bases of the columns were turned to account to afford a lofty standing room. And such a crowd! Earnest, intensest curiosity was marked on every face. The way it mingled with awe and devotion was at times rather ludicrous. Hands were clasped in prayer, and heads were bowed, and the lips were reciting something most devoutly; when up the head would be almost jerked, eye-glasses, spectacles, and, a little further off, opera-glasses and lorgnettes would be levelled at the reliquary for a minute or two; and then down with them, and again at the prayers. There were Frenchmen, Germans, Englishmen, Spaniards, and Americans; strangers of every nation. And these had made their way, of course, closest to the altar; at least they predominated in my vicinity. In the body of the chapel, the Neapolitans and Italians stood. The crowd reached to the railing under the grand archway, and beyond that filled the west aisle of the cathedral

church, and stretched across the nave and the east aisle to the chapels opposite The last stood nearly eighty yards off.

These Neapolitans, too full of faith and brimful of devotion on this day, and always exceedingly demonstrative in their manner, gave full way to their feelings, and were praying aloud or nearly so. The common people of Naples have a habit of modulating their voices while speaking, running up and down the gamut in a way quite novel to us. You heard those tones, not inharmonious, from the thousands who were praying in various pitches. Some were in groups, chanting or half-singing the litanies, some groups were reciting the rosary devoutly; others united in the acts of faith, hope, and charity; and still others in prayers and hymns appropriate for this occasion, and in their own Neapolitan dialect. To me it seemed a perfect Babel. But no one could for an instant look on them, and doubt the earnestness of their faith and the intensity of their devotion.

My attention was soon drawn to one group, or rather line, of a score of elderly women, from 50 to 80 years of age, strung along outside the sanctuary railing, from the centre door of it to the Gospel end. They all joined in one chorus. They all spoke so loudly, their tones were so earnest and modulated, and their position made them so prominent, that I asked who they were. I was told they were the ancient matrons of certain families in Naples who have ever claimed to be the blood-relatives of the saint; and, by right of prescription and usage, they occupy that position along the altar-rails on occasions of the exposition of the relics. They were evidently poor, very poor. It touched me to see here a dignity of descent claimed and recognized far beyond that based on wealth or worldly position—a dignity which nobles might crave in vain, and yet from which their poverty and daily drudgery do not debar these simple souls. I said they were old. Among them and close to them stood younger women and girls, other members, I presume, of their families, who at present prayed in lower tones, inaudible, or, at least, not noticeable, in the crowd of subdued voices When they become grandmothers, I presume they will take more prominent positions, and feel privileged to pitch their voices in shriller tones. I thought at first there was one exception. I heard a clear, bell-like, treble voice, which generally led their chorus of litanies or prayers, and which never seemed to tire. But I was mistaken in the supposition. I at last traced the voice. It was that of an elderly woman who will scarcely see sixty again She stood in the line, tall, thin, emaciated. Her brow was lofty; her eyes clear, and blazing with animation; her cheeks sunken in, not a tooth left; and, as she spoke, her broad chin seemed to work up and down a full inch. She wore a clean, old, faded calico gown, without any starch in it; and around her head was wound, like a turban, a bright, stiffened, red and yellow bandanna, reminding me somewhat of the respectable colored *maumas* I had seen in the South. Her voice was clear and sweet, and she made free use of it. Others might tire, or rest, or suspend their clamorous prayers for a while; but she, no, she never tired, and her voice was ever heard among the rest, like a clear trumpet stop in a full organ. It was delightful, at last, to watch her occasionally, as she kept her eyes fixed on the bust of the saint on the altar, and every feature of her countenance kept changing to express the sense of her words. Were she not in church, her hands and arms and whole body, I am sure, would have joined in the movements. As it was, she confined herself to bowing her head, or turning it slowly from side to side, yet always keeping her eyes fixed on the altar. I had seen, many times, earnest, silent, tearful prayer. Here I witnessed equally earnest, *noisy* prayer. I might come to like it, but only after some time and after many trials.

While this universal hubbub of prayer was filling the church, the chaplain, still holding the reliquary in his hands by the stem beneath, bent over the altar, and, with the other chaplains and those of the bystanders who joined in, recited the *Miserere* and other psalms, and the Athanasian Creed, and various prayers. His face glowed with the intensity of his feelings. He kept his eyes earnestly fixed on the reliquary, from time to time moving it over from side to side, and examining it. Sometimes he rubbed the glass face, front or rear, as necessary, with his white pocket-handkerchief, that he might see more clearly the interior. Sometimes the other chaplain held the candle in a proper position to aid his inspection. In about five minutes, he turned round with the reliquary to the people, and held it

up, with the candle behind it, that all might see. He let those near look as scrutinizingly as they wished, reached it to each one of the ten or fifteen on the platform and upper steps to kiss it, and, if they chose, as, of course, they did, to examine it, at six or ten inches distance. He then turned to the altar as before, and the litany of the saints was recited, with some other prayers. In about five minutes more, he again turned towards the people, and gave the immediate bystanders another opportunity to examine the reliquary closely as before. Then again to the altar for other psalms, hymns, and prayers. This alternation of prayers at the altar, holding the reliquary near the bust, and of presentations of it to the bystanders and the crowd, every five minutes or so, continued for over half an hour. But no change was visible. Once he left the altar, and making his way—I could not imagine how—into the crowd outside the sanctuary in the body of the chapel, gave to those to the right and left of his route a similar opportunity. On another occasion, he went down again; but this time he turned to the right, and went along the line of "relatives." How their fervor increased, how their demonstrations became more energetic, their words more rapid, their chorus fuller, their voices louder and shriller! He came back; but still no change. The alternations continued as before.

At last, a little after ten o'clock, I saw a change. I think I was the very first to perceive it. On all the previous times and up to this, the *ampulla* or vial was perfectly full, as I had seen it when first taken out of the armory. I now noticed a faint streak of light between the substance in the vial and the top, or, rather, the mass of solder into which the top of the vial entered. I was sure it had not been there before. I could scarcely see it now. This time, as on several other occasions, the chaplain came twice or thrice around the ring of immediate bystanders, those at first in front courteously giving way that others might in turn come forward. But I, of course, retained my place. As he came round the second time, and approached me again—I was within the line or semicircle—I saw that the streak of light was now clear and unmistakable. It caught the eye of an earnest little Frenchman who, for the last half-hour, had been pressing against me, at times rather inconveniently. He burst right out : " Don't you see the light in it? It is changing! It is liquefying!" The chaplain now looked at it attentively, moved it from side to side a little, rubbed the glasses with his white handkerchief, looked again, but went round the circle of by-standers a third time. Again he examined it. By this time the streak of light had become half an inch broad. He moved the reliquary from side to side slowly. We saw the vacancy now left above yield and follow his motions, just as the air-bubble does in a spirit-level, clearly showing the contents of the vial to be *now perfectly liquid.* Some looked on in silent awe; some shed tears; some cried out, "*Miracolo! miracolo!*" The chaplain waved his white handkerchief in signal that it really was so. Rose-leaves in quantities were thrown up from the crowd outside the sanctuary, and rained down on us. A dozen little birds that had been held captive in the baskets with the roses were liberated, and rose circling upwards to the windows of the dome. The grand organ burst out in the *Te Deum.* The vast crowd with one voice took up the hymn, almost drowning the full tones of the instrument. The bells of the cathedral tower, in full chimes, sent the announcement over the city, and the hills and valleys around, and over the quiet waters of the beautiful bay. All the bells of the other churches of Naples chimed in, and quickly the cannons of the Castle of Sant' Elmo joined in the chorus with a grand national salute.

Meanwhile, hundreds were approaching the altar to see with their own eyes that the blood was liquid, and to venerate the relics. Another chaplain now relieved the first, and continued to present the reliquary to those who were crowding up. I still retained my position. The blood continued to diminish in volume, until it sank so as to be a full half-inch below the neck of the vial. It was perfectly liquid, and, when the reliquary was turned or inclined, it ran off the up-raised sides of the *ampulla* at once leaving no more trace behind than would so much water.

After half an hour or so, the bust and the reliquary were carried in procession out from the chapel into the cathedral. The procession moved down the western aisle towards the doors of the church, turned into the grand nave, and advanced up to the sanctuary. The bust was placed on the high altar, and the canons of the cathedral replaced the chaplains of the *Tesoro* chapel in the duty of presenting the reliquary to the people, as they approached in undiminished numbers to venerate and inspect it.

At eleven, I said Mass at the altar where I had witnessed the liquefaction. After the Mass, I went into the church, and spent another half-hour there. Thousands pouring in from the streets were still flowing in a constant stream towards the high altar. A little after twelve, I left. . . .

Next morning, I said Mass again on the same altar at eight A.M., and before nine o'clock was again at the doors of the armories. Count C—— came punctually with his bag of keys. So did the little canon on the part of the archbishop. I was told that the sacred relics had remained exposed all day, after I left, on the high altar of the cathedral, the blood remaining liquid all the time; and that, about dark, they had, according to rule, been brought back to the *Tesoro* chapel, and had been locked up, as usual, for the night, in the armories. This morning, they were to be again brought out. Count C—— and the canon used their keys just as yesterday. The bust was taken out, and carried in procession to the front of the altar, as before. Then the other armory was opened, and the reliquary was taken out by the chaplain "It is hard, and at its ordinary level," he said, and showed it to us. The blood now stood in the *ampulla*, not, as yesterday, filling it, but reaching only to about an inch below the neck, leaving about one-fourth of the space within unoccupied. It was certainly solid and hard; for he turned the reliquary to one side and the other without its moving at all. He even held the reliquary upside down, and the blood remained a firm and unmoved mass, attached to the bottom of the now up-turned *ampulla.* It was carried to the altar. We stationed ourselves just as yesterday. The sanctuary was filled with visitors, but not so crowded as on the former occasion. The chapel, too, was not so densely jammed. None were forced to stand out in the church for want of room. The "relatives" were at their post, and prayed just as before, but the miracle having occurred on the feast itself, they were satisfied that it would occur, as a matter of course, each day of the exposition throughout the octave. At least, so I read their countenances, which were less nervously anxious than yesterday.

The chaplain commenced the *Miserere*, the *Deus tuorum militum*, and sundry prayers, the clergy joining in. Every five minutes or so, he turned to show the reliquary to the people, especially, of course, to those immediately around the altar.

In just sixteen minutes after we had reached the altar, the first symptom of the coming change showed itself. As the chaplain held the reliquary for a moment completely reversed, and steady in that position, I noticed that the surface of the blood within the *ampulla*, now, as he held it, underneath, showed a tendency to sag downwards, as if it were softening. Soon again, I saw that around the edge, where it touched the glass, it had changed color, and was of a brighter red than in the middle, and seemed very soft, almost liquid. In fact, as he would incline the reliquary to one side or another, the entire mass within began soon gradually to slide down and occupy the lowest position. Still, though soft, it was thick, and could scarcely be called liquid. Then, in two or three minutes more, it became still softer, until it was quite liquid, with a lump, nevertheless, which seemed to remain hard and to float in the liquid portion. To-day, as the glass was moved, the liquid would run off, of course. But, whereas yesterday it left the glass quite clear and clean, as water would do, now, on the contrary, it left a reddish thick tinge behind, which only slowly sank down into the general mass. After a while, too, the blood seemed to froth, or show bubbles on its surface—*to boil*, as the Italians say. I remained over half an hour more to see it, and I noticed that at the end of that time the lump had disappeared, and all was quite liquid. The frothing continued.

After this, I was invited to go .nto the sacristy, where they showed me the superb ecclesiastical vestments belonging to the chapel—the mitres, necklaces, chalices, ciboriums, ostensories, and other rich jewelry—in great part, the gifts of emperors, kings, and other nobles and wealthy ones, who, for centuries past, have given them as offerings to this sanctuary on occasion of their visits. Finally, I had to tear myself away. Returning for a few moments to the chapel, I found the crowds still approaching the altar to examine and to venerate the relics.

Reluctantly I left the cathedral, and in a few hours a railway-train was bearing me fast and far away from Naples.

I have thus, my dear S——, set forth minutely and at length what I saw. They say that in the liquid blood one may still sometimes see a small fragment of straw floating about. If so, it must have been taken up with the blood when it was gathered at the execution of the saint, and must have glided unperceived into the *ampulla* when the blood was poured into it that day. A young friend with me thought he caught a glimpse of it. His eyesight is keen, which, you know, mine is not. Anyhow, I did not see it. I need not tell you of various other little points of which the Neapolitans speak, as I had no opportunity of testing them or verifying them myself. I have told you, simply and straightforwardly, what fell under my own experience.

Our readers will not regret the length of this account of the liquefaction, so full and minute in the details. The letter from which we extract it was written immediately after the visit of the writer to Naples, from notes made at the time, and while the impressions left on his memory were still fresh.

It was not necessary, in a letter like that we have made use of, to enter on the discussion of mooted points of archæology. The writer simply sets forth the opinions which, after more or less of examination, he felt inclined to adopt. We say here that there is a difference among writers as to the year in which the body of St. Januarius was transferred from the original sepulchre to the church of San Gennaro *extra muros*, and there is still a graver difference as to the precise place of the original tomb. Some have held that the execution took place on a more elevated spot on the same hill which the letter mentions—about a quarter of a mile distant from the church of the Capuchins—and that this church marks not the site of the execution, as the letter holds with the Neapolitan archæologists, but the site of the first temporary interment, from which the body was borne to Naples, twelve or fifteen years later than the year assigned above. These are minor points, on which we may let antiquaries argue at pleasure.

In another article, we purpose to examine the character of the fact of the liquefaction of the blood of St. Januarius, according to exact records of its history for several centuries back.

For the present, we close with the latest account of its occurrence which has fallen under our eye. The *Pall Mall Budget*, of May 26 last, has the following: "The blood of St. Januarius seems to have been lately in a more perturbed state, if possible, than ever. The *Libertà Cattolica* of Naples gives an account of some unusual appearances presented by this relic, on the 6th inst., one of the annual occasions on which the holy martyr is honored in the cathedral of Naples. On the day in question,

Saturday, May 6, at a quarter-past four P.M., the reliquary being brought out of its tabernacle, where it had remained since the 16th of last December—the feast of the patronage —it was found partly liquid, as when laid up. It continued in the same state during the procession (from the cathedral to the church of St. Clara), and, after thirteen minutes of prayers, the sign of the miracle was given, the portion which had remained hard being perceptibly still more dissolved, so as to show that the miracle had taken place. Gradually, during the kissing of the reliquary by the congregation at St. Clara, it became entirely dissolved. On its return to the cathedral, contrary to what had taken place during the last few years, it was found to be completely hardened. When carried into the chapel of the *Tesoro*, it dissolved anew, and now entirely, yet remaining thick and glutinous; and in that state was laid up, about ten P.M."

II.

WHEN was this liquefaction of the blood of St. Januarius first seen by men ? It is not easy to answer the question. Some Neapolitan writers have maintained that it occurred probably on the very day when the remains of the sainted bishop were first solemnly transferred to Naples. For then, naturally and as a matter of course, the vials of the blood must have been brought into close proximity with the relics of the head. And this proximity, now intentionally brought about at each exposition, seems to be ordinarily the necessary and sufficient condition for the occurrence of the liquefaction. Others, however, prefer to be guided by positive historical evidence, and have come to a different conclusion. There is in existence a life of the saint written in or near Naples, about the year 920. It combines historical accounts and later legends, and evidently omits nothing which the writer thought would promote veneration toward the saint. It is diffuse on the subject of miracles. There is also in existence a panegyric of the saint, written perhaps half a century earlier still. No mention whatever is made in either of them of this Liquefaction. We may, therefore, conclude that in the year 920 it was not known. Four hundred and fifty years later, it was known, and had been known so long as to be reputed of ancient standing. About 1380, Lupus dello Specchio wrote the life of St. Peregrine of Scotland, who came to Naples about the year 1100, and died there probably about 1130. In that life it is stated that St. Peregrine came to witness this celebrated and continual miracle—*quotidianum et insigne miraculum.* Now, it may well be that the author, writing about two hundred and fifty years after the death of St. Peregrine, had access to documents and evidences clearly establishing this fact, although such documents do not now exist, five hundred. years later, or, at least, have not as yet been exhumed from some dusty library, where they may be lying unnoticed. Or, on the contrary, it may possibly be that in 1380 Lupus believed that the miracle, so regular in its occurrence at his day, had regularly occurred since the year of the translation of the body, and took it as a matter of course that St. Peregrine had witnessed it; and so put that down among the facts of his life. But this, even though a harsh criticism, and one we think unwarranted, if not excluded, by the words of the life, would imply at least that, in 1380, the Liquefaction had occurred for so long a time that men had ordinarily lost the memory of its commencement.

Maraldus the Carthusian, who accompanied his abbot Rudolph to the coronation of Roger, King of Sicily, as historiographer, tells us in his *Chronicon*—or perhaps his continuator—how, in 1140, Roger visited Naples, and how there he venerated the relics of the head and of the blood of St. Januarius. The Liquefaction is not mentioned in so many words. But these relics would not have been singled out from all others in the city, and made so prominent, without some special reason—a reason, perhaps, so well known and so obvious that it did not occur to the writer to state it explicitly, any more than to say that the king venerated the relics in the daytime and not at night.

The learned and critical Bollandists, who have carefully weighed all that can be said on this question, incline to hold that the Liquefaction commenced somewhere between the years 900 and 1000. Prior to the century between those years, St. Januarius had been ranked among the minor patrons of the church of Naples. After that century, he holds the most prominent place and rank in their calendar. This change is unusual and important, and must have been based on some sufficient reason. The most probable one under the circumstances—if not the only one that can be assigned—is that during that century the Liquefactions became known. The contemporary records of Naples for that time were very few; for it was a period of incessant warrings, devastations, and tumults. Those that did exist probably perished in the not unfrequent destruction of the monastic libraries. Still, some venerable manuscript may even yet come to light, telling us how on some festival day, or day of supplication, the relics were all on the altar, the vials of the blood near to the head; how some of the crowd that prayed before the altar saw that the blood in the vial had become liquid; how the wonderful thing was spoken of and seen by many; how, on other occasions, it occurred again and again; until at last it came to be regularly looked for, as a part, and the most wonderful part, of the celebration.

After 1400, the notices of the Liquefaction are more frequent. Æneas Sylvius Piccolomini (afterwards Pope Pius II.) gives an account of

it. Robert Gaguin, the old French historian, narrating the journey of Charles VIII. into Italy, mentions his visiting Naples in 1495, and his witnessing and examining this miracle of the Liquefaction.

In 1470, Angelo Catone, a physician of Salerno, who devoted the later years of his life to literature and to travelling, has written a brief but clear account of it. Picus de la Mirandola, the wonder of his age, has also left his testimony as an eye-witness.

It is needless to say that, since the invention of printing and the multiplication of books, we have numberless accounts of it from travellers and authors, in Latin, Italian, German, Polish, English, French, Spanish, and every language of Europe.

Ever since September, 1659—ten years after the opening of the new *Tesoro* chapel—an official diary has been kept in it, recording day by day the expositions of the relics; in what state and condition the blood was found when extracted from the *armoire*, or closet; after the lapse of what length of time the change, if any, occurred; what was its course and character; in what condition the blood was, when safely replaced in its closet in the evening; and, generally, any other facts of the day which the officers charged with this duty deemed worthy of note.

There are also printed forms in blank to the same effect, which one of them fills out and signs in the sacristy attached to the *Tesoro*, and distributes each day of exposition to those who desire them. We have several in our possession.

Another diary is kept in the archiepiscopal archives. It was commenced long before that of the *Tesoro*. We had an opportunity of looking over it. Down to the year 1526, it seems to be made up from previous documents and extracts from various authors. In 1526, it assumes the character of an original diary. Here and there come intervals during which it appears not to have been regularly kept on. These omissions would be supplied from other sources, when, after a time, the diary would be resumed. From 1632 it is complete. We have before us a manuscript abstract of it, from which we will quote hereafter.

The church of Naples celebrates three festivals of St. Januarius each year; the feast proper of the saint, commemorating his martyrdom; the feast of the translation, commemorating the transfer of his body from Marcian to Naples; and the feast of the patronage, a votive one of thanksgiving. We take them up in the order of time as they occur each year.

I. The first Sunday of May is the feast of the translation. On the preceding Saturday—the vigil, as it is termed—a solemn procession, during the forenoon, bears the bust containing the relics of the head of the saint from the cathedral to the church of Santa Chiara, or St. Clare. In the afternoon, another more imposing procession conveys the reliquary of the blood to the same church, in which the liquefaction is then looked for. About sunset, both relics are borne back in procession to the cathedral and *Tesoro* chapel, and at the proper hour are duly locked up. On the next day, Sunday, they are brought out, first to the altar of the *Tesoro* chapel, and thence, after a couple of hours, to the high altar of the cathedral. In the afternoon, at the appointed hour, they are again brought back to the *Tesoro* chapel, and are duly replaced in their closet, or *armoire*. The same is repeated on Monday, and on each succeeding day of the octave up to the following Sunday, inclusive. Thus, for this festival in May there are *nine* successive days of exposition. And, inasmuch as in the mind of the church the vigil, the feast, and the octave are all united together, as the celebration of one festival in a more solemn form, so we naturally look on those nine expositions not as isolated and distinct, one from the other, but as in some way connected together and united to compose a single group.

The feast and its vigil are found in ancient calendars of the church of Naples. The octave was added about the year 1646, on the occasion of completing and consecrating the new *Tesoro* chapel, the work and the pride of the city. The processions on the vigil were at first directed to such churches as the ecclesiastical authorities might from time to time select, to meet the convenience or the wishes of the faithful. In 1337, eight special churches were designated to which in an established order of succession the processions would thereafter go in turn each year. In 1526, it was stipulated between the city authorities and the archbishop that they should instead go in turn to six municipal halls, or *seggie*, as the Neapolitans styled them, belonging to as many civic bodies or corporations, which united, in some complex and ancient way, in the municipal government of the city: that is, to the chapels or churches attached to these *seggie*. This regulation was strictly followed until the year 1800. The old mediæval usages and liberties had by that time become weakened or had died out under the influence of modern centralization. The several old civic corporations of Naples, if they existed at all, existed only in name. The halls or *seggie* had lost their original importance and standing. A new regulation seemed necessary. From 1800 down, the procession of the vigil has gone each year to the church of Santa Chiara.

II. On the 19th of September occurs the Feast of St. Januarius, the chief or proper festival of the saint, commemorating his life of virtue and his glorious death by martyrdom under Diocletian. It is traced back to the earliest martyrologies and calendars of the church; even those of the Greek schismatic church have preserved it. In Naples, St. Januarius being the patron saint of the city, this festival is, of course, one of high rank, and has an octave. Opening on the nineteenth, and closing on the twenty-sixth of September, it gives each year *eight* days more, on each one of which the relics are brought forth about 9 A.M., and are placed on the main altar of the *Tesoro* chapel, and, about 11 A.M., are carried thence out to the high altar of the cathedral, whence again in the evening they are regularly brought back to the *Tesoro* chapel, to be replaced for the night in their proper closets. On each day, the liquefaction is looked for. The reason already given in the case of the May octave applies here also. These eight days of exposition are not eight isolated or distinct days, without any connection. They should rather be looked on as forming a second group.

III. On the 16th of December is celebrated the feast of the Patronage of St. Januarius. This is a single day festival in annual thanksgiving for many favors received, and especially for the preservation of Naples, two centuries and a half ago, from the fate of Herculaneum and Pompeii.

Naples lies almost under the shadow of Mount Vesuvius, that terrible volcano which, after slumbering peacefully for an unknown number of ages, renewed its fearful and destructive eruptions in A.D. 79, 203, 462, 512, and more than fifty times since. The burning gas or the smoke from its crater has risen miles into the air, and has spread like a dark cloud scores of miles on one side or the other. It has thrown up stones, which fell in showers of lapilli ten miles away. Its ashes have been borne to Tunis and Algiers in Africa, and to Tuscany, to Illyria, and to Greece in other directions. Once they clouded the sky and filled the air even in Constantinople. Streams of molten lava have flowed down its sides, filling valleys that were broad and deep, and sending in advance a sulphurous atmosphere and a glowing heat which destroyed all animal and vegetable life, even before the fiery stream itself touched plant, tree, or animal. They roll on slowly, but so inflexible and irresistible that no work or art of man can stay the movement or control its course. Everything in its path is doomed to utter destruction. *Resina*, between Naples and the mountain, has been destroyed and rebuilt, it is said, seven times; *Torre del Greco*, near by, nine times. Other places have perished as did Herculaneum and Pompeii. On every side of the mountain, so fair to look on when peaceful, so terrible in its wrath, one may follow for miles on miles these ancient currents, radiating from the centre. Here the hard, dark rock rings, as iron would, under your horse's hoof. There, what was once a death-bearing stream of lava has been covered by time with a rich soil, on which vines and olives flourish. By the shore, you may see where they reached the water, and have added leagues of rough volcanic rock to the land.

Naples has often been violently shaken, and sometimes seriously injured; has often been in imminent peril, but never was utterly destroyed. This brilliant capital, uniting in herself all that Italian taste admires of beauty and luxury—" *Vedi Napoli, e muori*"—lives with a sword of Damocles ever suspended over her. Each night as they retire the Neapolitans may shudder if they cast a thought on the possible horrors of the night they have entered on or what the morrow may bring them.

But men become callous even to such dangers as these, when often threatened and seldom felt. We can conceive how thoroughly all thought of them had died out in 1631, when Vesuvius, in a long unbroken sleep of one hundred and ninety-four years, had allowed six generations of Neapolitans to grow up and pass to their graves without any experience of its power. Earthquakes, explosions, flames, smoke, and streams of fire were all forgotten. Towns and villages, and gardens and vineyards, were dotting the base of the mountain or climbing its pleasant and fertile slopes. And among the many charming scenes in the neighborhood of Naples, there were then none more sweet and charming than those of the narrow tract between the city and Mount Vesuvius.

So it was on the morning of Tuesday, the 16th of December, 1631. Yet fair as was the scene on which the sun rose that day, it was to be greatly changed ere night. Early in the morning, the citizens were startled and somewhat alarmed by a very perceptible tremulousness of the earth under their feet. It increased in violence as the hours rolled on, and the atmosphere too, December though it was, became sultry and close. The inhabitants of the beautiful villas and the farmers and country laborers, who had felt the trembling of the earth and

the closeness of the atmosphere more sensibly than the citizens, and who saw at once that it was caused by the mountain, commenced to flee with their families for safety into the city. About 9 A.M. a cry of affright went up from the city and the country, as suddenly the mountain shook and roared as if in agony. All eyes turned to the summit of Vesuvius, only yesterday so fair and green. A huge turbid column of smoke was seen swiftly springing upward from its cone toward the sky. High up, it spread out like the top of a mighty pine or palm. The lightning flashed through this rolling, surging, ever-increasing mass as it rapidly expanded on every side. By 11 A.M., Naples lay under the dark and fearful cloud which shut out the heavens and darkened the day. The incessant trembling of the earth was perceptibly increasing in violence. Men felt that they were at the beginning of they knew not what terrible tragedy, before which they felt themselves utterly powerless.

The ever-open churches were soon crowded with fear-stricken suppliants. The cardinal archbishop at once directed religious services to be commenced in them all, and to be continued without intermission. In the hours of the afternoon there would be a procession through the streets near the cathedral, in which the relics of St. Januarius would be borne. Men prayed to be spared from the impending doom. The trembling earth might open to swallow them; the tottering houses might fall and crush them; or the mountain, whose sullen roar, like that of an angry monster, they heard amid and above all other sounds, might destroy them in some other more fearful way. They prayed and did penance, like the Ninivites of old. They sought to prepare their souls for the death which might come to many of them.

To the gloom and horrors of the dark cloud of smoke, spread as a funeral pall over the city, was added, later in the day, a pouring rain. The water came down heated and charged with volcanic ashes. Night arrived, more terrible than the day. The continuous trembling of the earth had indeed ceased; but, instead, there came sharp, quick shocks of earthquake, four or five of them every hour, vastly increasing the danger of those who remained in their houses. Out-of-doors was the pouring rain and the intense darkness, rendered more fearful by the intermittent electric flashings of the cloud overhead. The few oil-lamps in the streets gave little light; some had not been lighted, others had been extinguished. The narrow streets sounded with shrieks of alarm and prayers for mercy. They were filled with those who chose rather the darkness, the rain, and the mud under foot, than the danger within their own chambers. And all through the city might be descried entire families grouped together, and, by the light of torches or lanterns, making their way to some church—for, all through the terrible hours of that long night, the churches still remained open and thronged, and the services still continued. Day came at length, if the dim, misty light could be called day. It brought no relief beyond its saddening twilight. All hearts were depressed and filled with gloomy forebodings. All felt that only by the mercy of God could they be rescued.

At 10 A.M. there came two shocks of earthquake severer than any that had preceded them. The waters of the bay twice receded, leaving a portion of the harbor bare, and twice rolled back furiously, rushing over the piers and quays, and passing into the lower streets of the city. A hoarse and violent roar was heard from the mountain. It was soon known that the sea of lava within its bowels had burst for itself a channel-way out through the northern side, and was pouring down in a rapid stream, widening its front as it spread into seven branches, and advancing directly towards the city. *Portici* and *Resina*, near the mountain, or, rather, on its lower slope, were seen quickly to perish. Portions of Torre del Greco and of Torre dell' Annunziata shared the same fate. It seemed to the affrighted Neapolitans, as they looked on the fiery streams pouring onward, resistless and inflexible, in their course of destruction, that death was coming to them by fire, more terrible far than death by water or by earthquake.

Meanwhile, the hour at last arrived fixed for this day's procession. The archbishop was to take part in it, and would himself bear the reliquary of the blood of St. Januarius. The clergy of the city would precede and accompany him, and the municipal authorities would walk in procession behind. Thousands were in the cathedral and would follow after, and tens of thousands crowded the streets through which its route lay. A common feeling filled all hearts alike; they prayed earnestly, if ever they did—for their lives, and their homes, their all was at stake.

The rain had ceased, but the dark cloud still hung overhead, and the ashes were still falling, and the air was close and sulphurous. As the procession issued from the cathedral, and while the archbishop stood yet in the square in front of it, a blaze of sunlight beamed around. The sun itself they did not see, but his beams found some rift in the mass of smoke surging overhead, and struggled through, throwing, for a few moments, a glow of golden effulgence down on the cathedral and the square, and the groups that stood or knelt within it. The effect was electric. "It is a miracle! our prayers are heard!" was the cry that burst from the multitude. In a few moments the light was gone; but, with cheered and hopeful hearts, the procession moved on through the crowded streets to the gate of the city, looking directly towards Vesuvius and the advancing streams of lava. Here an altar had been prepared in the open air, psalms were chanted, prayers and litanies succeeded, and the archbishop, ascending the steps of the altar, stood on the platform, and, holding aloft the reliquary of the blood, made with it the sign of the cross towards the blazing mountain, and all prayed that God, through the intercession of their great patron saint, would avert the dreaded and dreadful calamity.

Ere the archbishop descended from the altar, all were aware that an east wind had sprung up, and that the smoke and cinders and ashes were being blown away over the sea. The mountain grew calmer, and at once ceased to pour forth such immense supplies of molten lava. The dreaded stream, no longer fed from the copious fount, soon slackened its movement—ceased to advance towards them—and, before their eyes, was seen to grow cold, and solid, and dark. When that procession, on its return, reached the cathedral, the sun was shining brightly and cheerfully. Well might they close with a solemn *Te Deum*, for Naples was saved. Outside of the city, five thousand men, women, and children had perished, and ruin was spread everywhere; within the city, not one building had fallen, not one life had been lost.

The eruption continued for some months after, but in a moderated form. The danger to the city was not renewed.

Therefore, in 1632, and in each year since, the sixteenth of December has been a memorable and a sacred day for Naples. It became the festival of the *Patrocinio*, or Patronage of St. Januarius. For a century and a half, it was kept as a religious holy-day of strictest obligation. But the sense of gratitude dies out equally with the sense of dangers from which we escaped in the distant past. Whether this was the cause, or whether it was deemed proper to yield to the so-called industrial notions that have prevailed in more modern times, we cannot say; but, for three-quarters of a century back, if we err not, this festival in Naples ranks only as one of devotion. For a number of years, its celebration was even transferred to the Sunday following. In 1858, it was transferred back to the day itself, and is now celebrated invariably on the sixteenth of December. On that day, the relics are taken from their closet and borne to the altar of the *Tesoro*, and thence to the high altar of the cathedral. After Mass, and the recitation of a portion of the divine office, they are borne in solemn procession through several streets in the vicinity of the cathedral, and, on the return, are brought again to the high altar, where there is the exposition of the relics with the usual prayers; and the liquefaction is looked for for the *eighteenth* regular time each year.

If the weather be rainy, the procession goes merely through the aisles and nave of the large cathedral and back to the high altar.

This feast has taken the place of another single-day festival, formerly celebrated on the fourteenth of January, and now merged in this votive feast a month earlier.

Beyond these ordinary and regularly established expositions, other special or extraordinary ones have been occasionally allowed, sometimes at the request of distinguished strangers, who visited Naples mostly in winter, and could not wait for the recurrence of the regular festival; sometimes to allow learned and scientific men, earnest in the cause of religion, to examine the liquefaction more closely and quietly than they could do amid the concourse of so many thousands on the regular days; and, sometimes, for special and urgent reasons of devotion or public need, as was that of December 16, 1631, of which we have just given the account. These extraordinary expositions were more frequent and more easily allowed two or three centuries ago than in later years. In fact, the latest one of which we can find any record occurred in 1702. Pope Pius IX. himself, during his exile in Gaeta, near Naples, waited for a regular day—September 20, 1849—to witness the liquefaction.

On a number of religious festivals during the year, it is customary to take out the bust of St. Januarius, containing the relics of his head, and to place it, with other relics of the saints kept in the cathedral, on the altar. To do this, it is, of course, necessary that the city delegate with his keys should be in attendance, and should co-operate with the canon or clergyman sent by the archbishop with his keys. Together they open the closet in which, under two locks, is kept the bust, and which, our readers will remember, is built in the massive masonry wall of the *Tesoro* chapel, immediately behind its main altar, and adjoining the similar closet in which is preserved the reliquary

with the ampullæ, or vials, of the blood. As this reliquary of the blood is not to be taken out on these occasions, its closet is ordinarily left untouched. But, in some rare instances, it has been opened, and due record made of the state in which the blood was then seen to be. At some other times, also, the door has been opened by special favor, that strangers might at least take a similar view, if they could not be present at an exposition. We have the record of nineteen times altogether since 1648, when the door was opened for one or the other of these reasons, the last time being June 11, 1775, when the blood was seen *hard*. However, as to the number of such minor examinations, we apprehend that we should speak with some hesitation. There may have been many more of which we have not just now at hand sufficient information.

We have spoken of the official diary of the *Tesoro* chapel, commencing in 1659, and of the archiepiscopal diary, commencing as a diary in 1526, and both continuing, the latter with some *lacunæ* in its earlier portions, down to the present time. Of course, different hands have penned its pages as years rolled on; and it is curious and amusing to note their differences of character as shown in their styles. Even in so plain a matter as recording, day after day and year after year, the state and condition of the blood when extracted from its closet, the occurrence and character of the liquefaction, the prominent or important facts of each day, and in what condition the blood was when replaced at night in its closet—points which it was the duty of all to record—personal traits are unwittingly manifested. One writer evidently was fond of ecclesiastical ceremonies, and he is exact in recording the character of the High Mass and of the processions : who and how many walked in them, how many altars were erected on the route through the streets, etc. Another was more of a courtier, and he carefully mentions the presence of cardinals, viceroys, ambassadors, princes, and eminent personages. A third was devoted to prayer, and his entries breathe his spirit of devotion in many a pious ejaculation. One tells you of a new musical *Te Deum* that was sung. Another had a painter's eye, and never fails to name, with minute precision, the varying shades of color seen in the blood. Another still, with more of a mathematical turn, is equally exact in setting forth to the very minute the times of the liquefactions which he records ; while others, again, performed their duty in a more perfunctory style.

On the whole, these diaries are to us most interesting and unique, as well for the length of time they cover, and the evident sincerity and earnestness of the writers in stating faithfully what they saw—sometimes to their own astonishment or sorrow, sometimes with joy—as also for the wonderful character of the facts themselves which are recorded.

Of the archiepiscopal diary, we possess a manuscript abstract, kindly written out for us. From its pages we have made a summary of all the expositions of the blood of St. Januarius at Naples from the year 1648 to 1860, which we present to our readers in tabular form. We group them together in octaves, for the reasons already given, and because in that form several peculiarities are clearly seen which, perhaps, otherwise would disappear.

We give, first, three tables for the vigil, feast, and octave in May. The first one shows the state of the blood when taken out from its closet, giving to each day a column, and recording in each column the various conditions of the blood, distinguishing them as : 1. Very hard ; 2. Hard ; 3. Soft ; 4. Liquid, with a hard lump in the liquid ; 5. Hard and full ; 6. Full, when, on account of that fulness, it could not be known whether the dark mass of blood within was solid or fluid ; 7. Liquid. A second table will set forth, under a similar arrangement, the various lengths of time which elapsed from the taking out of the reliquary of the *ampulla* from its closet until the liquefaction was seen to commence. After enumerating the instances in which the time is clearly determinable, another line indicates the times when the liquefaction is set down as gradual, sometimes because the time was not clearly seen, sometimes, perhaps, because the recording was perfunctory. We add another line, embracing the various occasions when the diary either omits recording or indicating the time, or does so, vaguely or in such terms as "*regular, very regular, promptly, punctually, most punctually, without unusual delay, without anything new.*" We subjoin to this table other lines, showing on what days and how often the blood remained always fluid ; or always fluid with a hard floating lump ; or always hard ; or always full, and so full that liquefaction was not detected. A third table, similarly arranged, will show in what condition the blood was when locked up at night in its closet. We also give three similar tables for the feast and octave of September, and similar accounts for the December festival and for the extraordinary expositions.

May, 1648, to May, 1860, inclusive—213 Years.

TABLE I.

STATE OF BLOOD AT THE OPENING OF THE CLOSET.

MAY.	Satur.	Sun.	Mon.	Tues.	Wed.	Thur.	Fri.	Satur.	Sun.
Very hard..............	2	....	1	1	2	....	2	2	2
Hard...............	156	119	207	203	168	139	123	113	113
Soft..................	4	8	1	3	2	5	3	7	6
Liquid, with hard lump..........	40	74	....	....	....	1	....	....	....
Hard and full.............	3	....	....	1	6	9	13	15	17
Full...................	....	....	....	4	33	56	68	75	73
Liquid..............	8	12	4	1	2	3	4	1	

TABLE II.

TIMES OF THE LIQUEFACTIONS.

MAY.	Satur.	Sun.	Mon.	Tues.	Wed.	Thur.	Fri.	Satur.	Sun.
Under 10 minutes.........	88	67	85	44	27	23	18	16	16
Under 30 "	49	23	63	73	46	46	44	35	37
Under 60 "	18	9	8	36	42	25	19	17	13
Under 2 hours..........	5	4	2	1	5	6	5	11	7
Under 5 "	1	7	....	....	2	2	2	3	3
Over 5. "	1	....	1	....	....	....	2	2	4
Gradual	1	40	....	....	....	1	....	....	....
Vague or omitted...........	26	45	54	55	54	52	51	53	56
Always liquid, with hard lump	17	1							
Always full..........	....	....	....	4	33	56	68	75	73
Always hard............	1	....	....	....	....	....	....	....	....
Always liquid............	6	12	....	....	4	3	3	1	2

TABLE III.

STATE OF THE BLOOD WHEN LOCKED UP AT NIGHT

MAY.	Satur.	Sun.	Mon.	Tues.	Wed.	Thur.	Fri.	Satur.	Sun.
Liquid	131	203	204	174	145	130	122	121	130
Liquid, with hard lump.......	77	10	4	....	....	....	....	....	....
Liquid and full..:..........	....	....	5	35	33	25	21	14	8
Full.....................	....	....	....	4	33	56	68	75	73
Soft...................	3	....	....	....	1	....	....	1	....
Hard	2	....	....	....	1	2	1	1	1
Hard and full............	....	....	....	....	....	....	1	1	1

These tables present the course of the expositions for two hundred and thirteen times each of the nine days, in all, 1,917 expositions. They do not set forth the changes in color, in frothing and ebullition, in minor increases or diminutions of volume, and in occasional hardenings, of all which we shall treat further on.

From September, 1648, to September, 1860—212 Years.

TABLE I.
STATE OF THE BLOOD ON OPENING THE CLOSET.

SEPTEMBER.	19	20	21	22	23	24	25	26
Hard	117	191	190	191	187	189	191	195
Hard and full, (*probable*)	24	....	....	....	....	....	....	...
Hard and full	58	....	....	....	....	2	1	1
Soft	1	....	1	....	....	1	1	....
Full	....	....	1	1	2	2	2	2
Liquid	12	21	20	20	23	18	17	14

TABLE II.
TIMES OF THE LIQUEFACTIONS.

SEPTEMBER.	19	20	21	22	23	24	25	26
Under 10 minutes	35	32	62	59	59	51	51	55
Under 30 "	64	101	78	76	78	83	79	84
Under 60 "	19	24	17	21	10	18	21	15
Under 2 hours	19	4	5	4	8	4	8	7
Under 5 "	27	....	....	1	1	2	2	....
Over 5 "	13	....	....	....	....	....	....	....
Vague or omitted	23	30	28	30	32	35	33	35
Always liquid	12	21	21	20	22	18	17	14
Always full	....	....	1	1	2	1	1	2

TABLE III.
STATE OF THE BLOOD WHEN LOCKED UP AT NIGHT.

SEPTEMBER.	1	20	21	22	23	24	25	26
Liquid	212	211	211	210	206	208	209	202
Liquid and full	....	1	....	1	3	3	2	8
Always full	....	....	1	1	2	1	1	2
Hard	....	....	....	....	1	....	....	....

These tables give two hundred and twelve expositions for each day, and thus for the whole group a second aggregate of 1,696 expositions. They do not, any more than the preceding ones, give an account of the changes to which the blood is subject, in color, frothing, or minor increase or decrease of volume. These points will be considered in their proper place.

The festival of the patronage on the 16th of December, established in 1632, has been celebrated 228 times down to 1860.

I. On opening the closet or safe the blood was found as follows:

Very hard,	2
Hard,	214
Soft,	1
Hard and full,	10
Liquid,	1—228

II. The variations as to times of liquefaction were as follows:

Immediately or under half-hour,	26
Under 1 hour,	99
" 2 "	41
" 5 "	42
Over 5 hours,	26
Always hard,	43
" full,	3
" liquid,	1
Vague or omitted,	17—228

III. The condition of the blood, when put up. was as follows:

Liquid, ... 131
   "   with lump, ... 46
Soft, ... 5
Hard as found, ... 43
Full, ... 3—228

The extraordinary expositions were 43 in number. Of these 20 may be grouped with the December exposition, having occurred in the months of November, December, January, and February.

The blood was found: Very hard, 1; hard, 13; soft, 5; and liquid, 1. The times of liquefaction were: Under 10 minutes, 15 times; under 30 minutes, 1; under 5 hours, 1; remaining liquid, 1. Of course, on all the 20 days it was put up liquid.

Nineteen days may be in the same way connected with the May celebration, as they are distributed through the months of March, April, May, and June.

The blood was found: Very hard, 1; hard, 13; soft, 4; liquid, 1. The times of the liquefaction were: Under 10 minutes, 10 times; under 30 minutes, 3; under 60 minutes, 1; under 2 hours, 1; under 5 hours, 1; time not indicated in the diary, 2; and it remained liquid, 1. On every occasion it was put up in a liquid condition.

Four other times there were extraordinary expositions in July and September. Twice the blood was found hard and liquefied within half an hour each time, and twice it was found liquid.

Nineteen instances are recorded in which for various reasons the closet was opened and the reliquary seen in its place. Four times the blood was found very hard; six times it was hard; twice it was soft; four times it was liquid, and three times the condition is not recorded.

These tables present an aggregate of no less than 3,884 expositions within a little more than two centuries, of which number no less than 3,331 were marked by a complete or partial liquefaction. The exceptions are of various classes. The most numerous one comprises 320 cases, in which the ampulla, or vial, was found in the morning and continued during the entire exposition of that day so completely full, that it was impossible for an ordinary observer to say whether the blood liquefied or not.

The writer of the diary says on this point, A.D. 1773: "When the vial is full, some signs are at times observed indicative of a liquefaction, chiefly a wave-like motion when the vial is moved. But as this can only be seen from the rear (that is, as the light shines on it or through it from the opposite side), and only on close inspection and by practised eyes, and is not visible to ordinary observers standing in front, it is not here noted down as a liquefaction." In the diary of the *Tesoro* chapel, which we cannot now consult, they are probably recorded as liquefactions.

The next largest class of exceptions consists of the 171 cases in which the blood was found liquid in the morning, and was replaced in the closet in the evening still in a liquid condition. We should observe that not unfrequently in such cases the fluid mass became congealed or even hard during the day and liquefied again. Even when this does not happen, there are so many other and frequent changes as to color, to frothing, or to ebullition, and to change of volume by increase or decrease, that, even without the occurrence of liquefaction, the fluid blood presents many wonderful characteristics. Thus in our synopsis we have counted the octave of September, 1659, as presenting seven days during which the blood was found and remained liquid

The diary, taking up that octave day by day, states, that on the 19th of September the blood was found liquid, and, the reliquary being placed near the bust, there commenced an ebullition of the blood marked with froth. This continued, off and on, during the day. On the 20th the blood was again found liquid, and the ebullition and the frothing were repeatedly renewed as on the preceding day. On the 21st the blood was a third time found liquid, and on this day the ebullition was more continuous and violent. The 22d and the 23d and the 24th were marked by the same phases. The blood was always found liquid, and each day the ebullition was repeatedly resumed and sometimes was violent. On the 26th the blood was found in a soft or jelly-like state. It soon liquefied entirely, and during the day became covered with froth. The 26th —the eighth and last day—was like the first. The blood was again found liquid, and the ebullition was resumed, yet more moderately.

The two remaining classes, which our tables present as exceptions, will also suffer diminution if accurately examined. There are 44 instances in which the blood was found *hard*, and continued hard to the end of the exposition. Yet the diary records on several occasions the presence of one or more fluid drops, sometimes of yellowish serum, sometimes of reddish blood, which could be made to run to and fro on the surface of the hardened mass, and continued to be seen for hours, or sometimes even until the close of the day.

As for the 18 other instances in which the blood was found partly liquid and partly solid, the solid part floating as a globe in the fluid portion, and in which the same state of things was seen during the day and lasted until the closing, it must be observed that generally, if not always, this floating solid mass gradually diminishes by a partial liquefaction or increases in bulk by a partial hardening. Sometimes both these changes succeed each other during the day. In view of these facts, it would seem that these 18 cases, so far from being looked on as exceptions, should on the contrary be rather set down as special forms of the liquefaction.

No mere tabular summaries, like those presented above, can give the salience which they demand to certain unusual facts and to many ordinary but striking characteristics which should not be overlooked. For this it is necessary to go back to the diaries themselves, and to trustworthy historical notices of the miracle.

On Saturday, May 5, 1526, the vigil of the feast of the translation, the liquefaction is recorded to have taken place as usual in the *Seggia Capuana*, to which the processions were directed that day. On the next day, the feast, the blood was found hard, and it continued hard during the entire exposition. The octave had not yet been established. It continued hard all through the octave of the succeeding September, as also in January, May, and September of 1527, and again in January, May, and September of 1528, and in January, 1529. The liquefactions were resumed on Saturday, May 1, and continued on the next day, the feast, and regularly during the September celebration. Thus, for nearly three years the blood remained hard and solid, without liquefying at any time.

The Neapolitans connect this unusual fact with the anger of God and his judgments, as manifested in the terrible pestilence which broke out in their city in 1526, and came to an end only in the early months of 1529, after causing 60,000 deaths in the single year 1527, and, together with the war then raging, as many more in the ensuing year 1528.

Again, in 1551, in 1558, and in 1569, there was no liquefaction. On the contrary, for the two years 1556 and 1557, and again for the two years 1599 and 1600, and a third time for the single year 1631, the blood was always found liquid when brought forth for exposition, and never at any time was seén to become solid. Since the last-named year, it has occurred, in ten different years, that the blood was found and continued liquid during the whole of a single octave in a year; but never in both octaves. It never continued hard for an entire octave at any time, although at some few times the liquefaction occurred only on the second, the third, or the fourth day of the celebration; or, on the contrary, it was found and continued liquid for one, two, or three days at the commencement, and was found hard only on the second, third, or fourth morning. At the votive festival of December 16, it has repeatedly remained hard. The table numbers 44 such cases. Of these only 5 occurred in the first 150 years after the institution of the feast; the remaining 39 all occur in the last 78 years. This the Neapolitans explain by the special character of the festival. The other festivals have been instituted in honor of the saint; this one, to show their gratitude as a city for favors received repeatedly through his intercession. Hence, when vice is rife in the city, and especially when sins against religion abound, their professions of gratitude are wanting in the most necessary quality to make them acceptable; and the displeasure of heaven is marked by the withholding of the miraculous liquefaction.

Departures like these from the ordinary course, or any extraordinary delay in the liquefaction, or certain appearances of color in the blood, which they traditionally dread, fill the people with alarm and sorrow. From the many instances in the diary we give two, as showing this practical connection between the liquefaction and the religious feelings of the Neapolitans.

"1732, Dec. 16.—The blood was taken out, hard. Hard it continued until after compline (the afternoon service). The people were waiting for the miracle with great anxiety. Wherefore, instead of taking back the relics (to the *Tesoro* chapel) at the usual hour, they remained on the high altar (of the cathedral) until after 21 o'clock (2.30 P.M.); and the church being crowded with people, they recited the litanies several times. Rosaries were said, and sermons were preached. But the saint did not yield, which caused great terror; and everybody was weeping, So things were up to 24 o'clock (5.30 P.M.) At that hour, a Capuchin father in the church again stirred up the people to sincere contrition for their sins, and to acts of penance. While they were doing this, all saw that the blood was of a sudden entirely liquefied—a great consolation to all. The *Te Deum* was sung; and then, only at half-past one of the night (7 P.M.), the relics were taken to the *Tesoro* chapel."

"1748, May 7, Tuesday.—The blood was brought out hard. After 16 minutes, it liquefied. During the day it rose so high as to fill the vial completely. From the 8th to the 12th, the vial was always full, and the blood was seen to be one-half black, the other half ash-colored, for which reasons his majesty came a second time to see it, on Sunday afternoon (12th). When the king had left the *Tesoro*, his eminence returned to pray to the saint to vouchsafe some sign of the miracle before the closing up (it was the last day of the octave). In the meantime the vast crowd strove to melt him by their cries and their tears. His eminence, having made his way out of the chapel with great difficulty, sent for a noble Capuchin, called Father Gregorio of Naples, who, in a most fervent sermon, exhorted the people to acts of faith and of sorrow for their sins. He then commenced reciting with them the Litany of the Blessed Virgin. During the recitation thereof, the blood was seen to sink half a finger, and to commence to move. Who can describe the weeping and the fervor? The *Te Deum* was sung; and the blood was put up, being at nearly its normal level, of its natural color, and with some froth."

No wonder the Neapolitans love St. Januarius as *their* patron saint when he thus yields to their fervent entreaties and prayers what was not granted to the pious curiosity of the king; nor, for this occasion at least, to the prayers of his eminence the cardinal archbishop.

The following briefer entries of our diary breathe the same spirit:

"1714, May 5, Saturday.—The miracle took place at once. On Sunday, after an hour and a half. During this octave, the blood showed a thousand changes, liquefying, hardening, and increasing in volume many times a day, in an unusual manner. God knows what will happen!"

"1718, Sept. 19.—The blood was taken out hard. After a quarter of an hour, it completely liquefied. During all this octave the miracle never delayed as much as an hour. This was truly a happy octave. There were no great changes; only a slight increase in volume."

It is tantalizing to pore over the diary. At times you almost fancy that you have seized the very process of liquefaction. Thus on one day you read: "The blood was brought out, being hard and at its ordinary level. After fifteen minutes, a drop of serous humor, of a light-yellow color, was seen to move about on the hard mass. At the expiration of an hour and fifty-six minutes, the blood became liquid, with a large spherical lump floating in it. There was the usual procession through the streets, his eminence joining in. At 21½ o'clock (about 3 P.M.) the lump liquefied. The blood was put up, entirely liquid and at its ordinary level." (Dec., 1771.) You think you see the steps of the process. First the drop of yellowish serum; then a partial liquefaction, leaving a lump of solid matter; this gradually decreasing for three hours and a half, until it entirely disappears, and the whole mass is fluid. If you read the following, you may feel surer that you are on the right track: "The blood came out hard and at its ordinary level. At the end of half an hour, there was seen to run about on the hard mass a particle of serous matter, inclining to a yellowish color. So it stood during the procession, which was outside, through the streets, his eminence the cardinal archbishop taking his place in it. So it was when the reliquary was brought back to the *Tesoro*. At 23½ o'clock (about 5 P.M.) this serous matter changed into blood. But the mass still remained hard. Words cannot tell with what earnestness and fervor the ecclesiastics and the people continued at prayer. Finally, at 24¼ o'clock (5.45 P.M.) the mass loosened in the vial; and half an hour later, that is, after eight hours and fifty minutes of waiting, the liquefaction took place, a small lump remaining solid and float-

ing. So it was put up." (Dec., 1768.) Notwithstanding the change of the character of the yellowish serous drop in the last cited instance into red blood, and the great difference of the times when the liquefaction took place, there is a certain degree of correspondence between the two cases—enough perhaps to arrest the attention and excite expectations. But all to no purpose. Such a drop was seen on seven or eight other days, lasting a couple of hours or for the entire day, without any liquefaction following. And in three thousand three hundred and odd cases of liquefaction, we have failed to find a third one in which such a drop is noted to have preceded the liquefaction.

In fact, the modes of liquefaction are as various as we can imagine, and as remarkable as the fact itself. Sometimes the liquefaction occurs or commences at once, with little or no delay. At other times, it is delayed for a quarter or for half an hour, for one, two, or three hours or more. Sometimes, though very rarely, it has been delayed nine or ten hours. All this is clearly seen in the tables.

Not unfrequently the change from solidity to fluidity, whether occurring early or late, has been instantaneous, and for the whole mass at once—*in un colpo d'occhio.* Sometimes it is gradual, lasting before its completion over many hours; nay, sometimes the ampulla is replaced in the closet for the night before its entire completion, a greater or a smaller portion still remaining solid.

Sometimes the entire mass liquefies; at other times, only a portion. When this is the case, the unliquefied portion generally floats as a solid lump or globe in the liquid part. Sometimes, however, one side of the mass was liquefied; while the other remained solid, and firmly attached to the glass. Sometimes again, as in May, 1710, the portion next to the glass all around remained solid, thus forming, as it were, an inner cup, inside of which the other portion moved about in quite a fluid condition. Sometimes, during the process of gradual liquefaction, the upper part is quite liquid, while the lower part remains for a time hard and immovable in the bottom of the vial; or, again, the lower part liquefies first, and the upper portion, remaining hard, is seen either as a floating globe or as a lump attached for a time to the sides of the ampulla. And once, at least, the upper portion and the lower portion both remained solid and attached to the vial, while the middle portion was quite fluid.

We have already said something of the various degrees of liquefaction. Sometimes the blood is as fluid as water, flowing readily and leaving no coating after it on the glass. And, at other times, it may be somewhat viscous; and, if the reliquary be inclined from side to side, may leave behind a dark or a vermilion film on the inner sides of the ampulla.

There are likewise degrees of hardness. Sometimes the blood is only very viscous and grumous, or jellylike. In the tables we call it *soft.* At other times, the diary notes it as hard, *duro ;* very hard, *durissimo ;* or even hard as iron, *duro come ferro.* When hard, it is attached firmly to the glass ampulla. Yet on two occasions, at least, the hard lump could move within, showing that it was then detached.

After having become liquid, or even when the blood was found liquid in the morning, it has often hardened during the ceremonial of the day, and then liquefied anew. One of the extracts we have quoted above refers to the frequent occur rence of this variation in 1714. But throughout the diary we find similar instances, where it hardened and remained hard for a few moments only or for one or two hours, during the public ceremony. This was sometimes repeated two or three times in a single day.

There is a special case, in which the mass hardens so frequently, and with such regularity, that it must not be omitted. We refer to the custom of suspending the ceremony for a few hours during the middle of the day. The Italians are very fond of a *siesta* in the early afternoon of a hot and oppressive summer day. Accordingly, unless there be something unusual to excite them, they are accustomed, on the later days of the octave in May, and sometimes of September, to yield to their beloved habit. The church grows very thin soon after mid-day. A few dozen pious souls may perhaps remain for their private devotions—about the number one would almost always find in the ever-open churches of an Italian city. Under these circumstances, the exposition is suspended. The reliquary, if on the high altar of the cathedral, is carried back to the *Tesoro* chapel, and is placed on an ornamental stand or tabernacle on the altar; and a silk veil is thrown over the whole. The door in the metal-work railing under the arch leading out into the cathedral is locked; and the clergy may retire, one or two remaining on watch. The reliquary continues on the stand, unapproached, but still visible, through the railing, to those in the cathedral. At 3½ or 4 P.M. the clergy return to resume the exposition; and the church is again full. The blood is very frequently found hard at that hour, and liquefies anew, as in the morning. This intermission and the attendant hardening and liquefaction seem to the Neapolitans so much a matter of course that we find no mention whatever of it in the diary, save the single notice that, on one day, although the veil had been omitted, the hardening nevertheless took place. The scientific men from Italy and from France and Belgium who have studied the liquefaction at various dates, all unite in commenting on this fact of the hardening of the blood during these mid-day intermissions, and in considering it, under a physical point of view, as a fact of the highest importance in deciding the character of the liquefaction.

There are other special circumstances under which the blood has not liquefied, or, having liquefied, has suddenly hardened again. The presence of open scoffers, or of declared enemies of the church, has sometimes seemed to have this effect. In 1719, Count Ulric Daun was viceroy in Naples. On Saturday, May 6, he came with many German officers lately arrived in Naples to witness the liquefaction, in one of the churches to which the procession went, as we have already explained, and in which the liquefaction was first expected. The viceroy with his personal staff was of course in his official *loggia* or gallery. The foreign officers were clustered together within the sanctuary. Some of them were Catholics, some Protestants. The blood was hard when brought to the altar, and remained hard and unliquefied for a long time. The viceroy at length sent an aid, with a command to all the officers to withdraw and stand outside the sanctuary. They obeyed, of course. "Scarcely was this done—the heretic officers thus withdrawing—when, in an instant, the entire mass became perfectly liquid, to the great joy of all. It was a miracle of miracles!" Some of the Protestants became Catholics immediately.

Putignani and *Celano* mention another fact. We quote from the former, who was a canon of the cathedral and present at the time on service. "While the relics were out at the high altar of the cathedral, there came many nobles from beyond the Alps, who wished to do homage to the saint and to witness the liquefaction. The blood was extremely fluid just then, and the reliquary was being presented to those around, in turn, to be kissed. In an instant the blood became hard and dry in the hands of the canon. Those near by, stupefied by this new prodigy, stood, as it were, nailed to the floor. Then the canon, moved by an interior impulse, raised his voice, and said aloud: 'Gentlemen, if there be any heretic among you, let him retire.' Immediately, one of the strangers quietly withdrew. Scarcely had he withdrawn, when the blood was liquid again, and was bubbling." Putignani adds: "The same thing is said to have happened on other occasions."

III.

But this is far from being the general rule. In 1543, the diary mentions the presence of Muleasses, Bey of Tunis, a Mohammedan, and records his expression of astonishment at what he beheld. On several other occasions, Mohammedans were witnesses of it; some became Christians. Protestant travellers from England, Denmark, Sweden, and Germany have written accounts of what they themselves saw. On four of the six occasions when the writer of these lines was present, he can bear personal testimony to the presence of Protestants.

It is narrated that the liquid blood has been known to solidify instantly, whenever the reliquary passed into the hands of a particular canon, in his turn of office, to be presented by him to the people, or when certain persons approached to venerate and kiss it, and would as quickly liquefy again when they withdrew. A notorious case is mentioned by the Bollandists, and by other authorities, of a prince, whose name, for family reasons, was not given—for the matter was published in his lifetime. At his approach the liquid blood used to become solid. His personal character left no doubt on the minds of the Neapolitans why this happened.

We have already spoken of the notable differences of color, on various days, or parts of the same day. The diary registers them as *bright, beautiful, vermilion, rubicund,* or as *dense* or *dark,* or *blackish,* or *ash-colored,* or, again, *pale* or *yellowish.* Sometimes the whole mass was of one uniform tint. Sometimes there were several tints in different parts, as in 1748, when, as we saw, one portion was blackish and the other ash-colored, the vial being then full, and the blood liquid, as afterwards appeared.

Again, the liquid blood is sometimes quite quiescent, yielding, indeed, to every movement of the ampulla, as water would, but when the ampulla is at rest on its stand, remaining in it as tranquil as water, with a level and smooth surface, and without the least indication of internal movement. Yet often it gives forth a froth or foam, which covers a part or all of the surface, which stains the glass dark or vermilion, and the remains or traces of which may be noticed on the mass when indurated afterwards; that is, if this foaming has continued until a solidification on the altar, or until the reliquary is locked up in the evening. Very often this foaming will cease after lasting half-an-hour or an hour. Its ending and disappearance is as fitful as its beginning.

Sometimes the motion is greater, and of a different character—an ebullition or boiling, as the Italians call it. Portions of the liquid blood are thrown up a quarter of an inch, or more. Sometimes this bubbling has been very violent, some of the liquid being thrown up into the neck of the ampulla to the very top.

On December 16, 1717, it is recorded that, before the liquefaction took place, and while the blood was still hard and solid, " an exhalation was seen to rise from the hard mass, like to a little cloud, and to ascend to the top of the neck." On 24th September, 1725, "the blood was taken out hard, and immediately liquefied; and three or four times, of itself, it moved round in a circle within the ampulla, although the ampulla was then in its place on the altar, and motionless."

It is needless to cite any more of the thousand-and-one items of such character scattered through the diary. They all show the sincerity and good faith of the writers, and the care with which the minutest facts were observed, and accurately recorded on the day of their occurrence.

Next to the occurrence of the liquefaction, the most important fact, in our judgment, is the frequent change of volume which the mass undergoes while liquid. We say while liquid, for we do not discover, either in the diary or in our researches elsewhere, any indication of such a change taking place while the blood is in its solid condition. But, while liquid, such changes are so frequent and so great that the diary, as we saw, noticed their absence or *quasi*-absence, during one octave, as something remarkable. The blood is said to be at its ordinary or normal level when it fills about four-fifths of the space in the ampulla, or vial. It has been known to sink below this, but very rarely. Ordinarily it is oscillating in volume, sometimes reaching the neck, or entering it so high as to leave only a thread of light, or even filling the neck up to where it enters the mass of soldering. The extreme distance between the two levels is about an inch and a half, and the volume must increase over twenty per cent. in order to rise from the ordinary level so as to fill completely the ampulla. The days are comparatively rare when

some change of volume is not seen, either by increase or by decrease. The change is generally gradual, yet such as may be watched and followed. Sometimes, however, it is quite rapid in the ascent or the descent, or in its alternations of rising and falling; sometimes almost instantaneous —*in un colpo, in un tratto.*

These ordinary oscillations or changes of volume, which occur at any time, may be looked on as the usual and minor form of one general and striking trait or mode of action. When the increase is carried to its utmost extent, the vial is seen to be completely filled; and this fulness, in turn, presents many variations to be studied. We may divide them into two classes. The first embraces all those cases in which the fulness terminates, and the blood commences to diminish in volume, at any time before the close of the octave; we may call these completed periods. The second embraces all those in which the fulness continues to the end, so that, on the last day of the octave, the blood is replaced in its closet still completely filling the ampulla; these we call incomplete periods.

To the prior class belong, first, all those many instances in which the blood swelled up and filled the ampulla and commenced to sink again in volume on the same day, whether after a few moments or after several hours of fulness. Again, the diary records *three* cases in which it so rose one day and sank the next; *four* cases in which it rose one day and sank the second day after, keeping the ampulla completely full for the entire intermediate day; *six* cases in which there were two such intermediate days; *two* with three, and *four* with four such intermediate days of complete fulness. We have thus nineteen cases recorded in the diary, to which we should add, perhaps, an equal number for the first category. A complete period, so to call it, of the fulness may vary, therefore, from a few moments to five consecutive days.

The second class comprises ninety-four instances of fulness opened and not completed during the octave. The varieties in these are even greater than in the former class. In *nineteen* cases the fulness, or, at least, its last phase, commenced on the closing day; in *five* cases, on the day before; in *nine*, on the third last day; in *eleven*, on the fourth; and in *twenty-two* on the fifth day, counting from the closing of the octave; in *twenty-six* cases, the fulness began on the sixth day; and in *two* cases, as far back as the seventh day, counting from the close of the octave. We have here twenty-eight of these incomplete periods, longer than the longest of the closed or complete periods, just mentioned, still further complicating any question as to the lengths of these periods of fulness.

Whenever, during an octave, the ampulla is locked up at night *full*, it will be found *full* the next morning. When it is locked up at the close of an octave in that state, it will be found in the same at the first opening of the next celebration, months afterwards. We said that the mass changed its volume only when in a fluid condition. We may now venture to add that such changes take place only in public, and never while the blood is closed up in the closet, or *armoire*. In examining the diary very carefully, we find that, in the vast majority of cases, the level of the mass as stated when taken out—whether it be at the ordinary level, or somewhat elevated, or very high, or full—perfectly agrees with the level at which it was

stated to stand when last put up, whether the day before or at the close of the preceding octave. In a number of cases, indeed, the diary is silent or obscure on the point; but its language often seems to imply this fact, or to take it for granted. Nowhere does it state the reverse in general terms; and we cannot find a single instance recorded which establishes the contrary. The blood is always found at the level at which it stood when last put up.

These ninety-four unclosed periods were, therefore, prolonged to the next festival, when the ampulla was taken out still *full*. Some of these periods had just commenced on the last day; others had lasted six full days after the day of their commencement. Is there any marked difference in their closing? Not in the day; for they all, with three exceptions, closed on the first day of the incoming octave, if they had run over to May or September, or on December 16, if that was the next exposition. In regard to time, there is no rule. The most numerous class, containing twenty-six instances, varied from *immediately* to *nine hours and a half;* nine times the liquefaction occurred in less than one hour, and nine times it delayed more than three hours—the other eight times it lay between the two. The twenty-two cases of the next highest class present the same diversities of time, from *immediately* to *nine hours and a half.* Nine instances were under an hour, eight were over three hours, the remaining five lay between the two divisions.

The more those periods of fulness are examined, the more clearly does it appear that they follow no system, and can be classified or accounted for by no law. We see the mass swelling and increasing its volume and filling the ampulla, and continuing to fill it for some moments, or hours, or days. We can note the facts; but why this increase? why does it rise so high? why to-day, and not yesterday, or to-morrow? why so long, or not longer? Physical science is as utterly unable to answer these questions as it is to assign a cause for the liquefaction itself, or for the various and varying phases of the blood of St. Januarius.

As was stated in our preceding article, the Neapolitans hold that the proximity of the relics of the head and the reliquary with the vials of the blood to each other, is ordinarily the sufficient and determining cause of the liquefaction. Their whole ritual of the expositions is based upon this principle. The separation of the relics, or their *quasi*-separation, by a veil thrown over the reliquary of the blood, is ordinarily sufficient to terminate the liquefaction and to indurate the blood anew. But, on the other hand, the diary records a number of instances in which the blood, having been found hard, liquefied at once, even before the reliquary was placed near the bust. Several times, too, it has liquefied in the streets, while carried aloft in the afternoon procession of the vigil in May towards Santa Chiara or a *seggia*, although the bust had already been carried thither in the forenoon. So, too, a liquefaction, partially commenced in the *Tesoro* chapel or in the cathedral, has often continued or been completed during the outdoor procession through the streets, on the festival of the patronage, in December.

Another cause or condition, perhaps as important as the proximity of the relics, is, in our judgment, the strong faith and the earnest devotion of the attendants—a faith and devotion in which the Neapolitans, clergy and people, are not surpassed. It

was, perhaps, for this reason, that in the extraordinary expositions of which we have spoken, the liquefaction so often occurred quickly, and, as the Neapolitans would say, *Il miracolo era bellissimo.* The devout strangers to whom the favor was granted brought to it faith and piety. On the few occasions when it was tardy—on none did it entirely fail—there may have been too strong an ingredient of mere profane curiosity. Kings, and princes, and nobles of high worldly standing have often visited Naples, and sometimes sought and obtained this favor of an extraordinary exposition of the relics in their presences, that, apart and with less danger of any intrusion on their personal dignity or comfort, and in the company of their chosen attendants only, they might have an opportunity of witnessing the miracle at their ease. This was the length of their privilege. As for the liquefaction itself, they had to wait as others waited, and, perhaps, because they did not pray as others prayed, they were sometimes disappointed.

In 1702, Philip V., King of Spain, to whom Naples was then subject, visited the city, reaching it on the afternoon of Easter Sunday. On Easter Tuesday, April 18, he was present at a Pontifical High Mass celebrated in the cathedral. After that long ceremony, his majesty passed into the *Tesoro* chapel, where there was to be a special exposition of the relics, that he might venerate them and might witness the liquefaction. "The blood was brought out hard; four Masses were celebrated in succession (about two hours); but the saint was not pleased to work it. The king departed, and the Masses continued. At the sixth Mass, and as the king had entered his carriage at the cathedral door, the blood liquefied. The king returned at 22 o'clock (3.30 P.M.), and kissed the relics in the hands of his eminence in the *Tesoro.*"

However, the diary mentions that he did witness the liquefaction itself at the next regular day in May, with all the people.

Other instances are given in which viceroys and nobles and princes waited until they were tired out. Soon after their departure, when the faithful and fervent people might freely crowd the chapel and pray, the liquefaction would occur.

It is impossible to exaggerate the firmness of their faith or the depth and tenacity of the affection of the Neapolitans for this *their* miracle. Whatever else happens to their fair city, nothing must interfere with their devotion to St. Januarius and the proper celebration of these festivals—neither wars nor pestilence, nor eruptions nor earthquakes, nor change of rulers. Once a battle raging in the streets prevented an outdoor procession. But, within the cathedral, there was a procession through the aisles and nave, and all things else went on as usual.

Oddly enough, the greatest disturber, to judge by the simple-minded writers of the diary, has been—rain. Not that the weather has any direct influence on the liquefaction or its circumstances. Quite the contrary. The blood liquefies all the same, and with as many attendant variations, whether the day be fair or rainy, whether the season be so dry that the farmers are complaining of drought, and prayers have been ordered for rain, or whether it has been raining incessantly for weeks and months, to the injury of the crops, and in the churches they are praying for fair weather; in summer, when the sun is pouring down his almost tropical beams; and in winter, when the procession is confined to the cathedral because it is too cold to go out into the streets, or because the ground is covered with snow. These meteorological changes have no apparent influence on the liquefaction or its characteristic circumstances.

But at Naples they sometimes have terrible deluges of rain—steady downpourings such as one may witness only within or close to the tropics. Sometimes these have come on just at the hour to interfere with the grand afternoon procession of the vigil in May, forbidding it, or ludicrously disarranging it, and forcing monks, friars, priests, seminarians, canons, and people alike to break the ranks and seek immediate shelter in the neighboring shops and houses. However, come what might, at the worst, his eminence, or the highest ecclesiastical dignitary present, with a few attendants of waterproof hearts, would carry the relic, in a sedan chair or a carriage, it might be, to the appointed place. Is it not all punctually set down in the diary; at what corner, or in what street, the procession was broken up, and who then carried the relic on, and whether still on foot or in a carriage, and how many courageously accompanied him? We may be sure that on arriving at their destination they never failed to find the church, despite the rain, and despite the absence of fashionable ones, filled by devout souls, who loved their saint more than they feared even such weather.

Passages in the extracts we have made from the diary, and many other passages we might quote, indicate the feelings of alarm which fill the hearts of the Neapolitans when the liquefaction fails to occur, or is attended by circumstances which they traditionally dread. St. Januarius is their patron saint. This ever-recurring liquefaction is, in their eyes, a perpetual and miraculous sign or evidence of his care and protection. When it occurs regularly, when the liquefaction is complete and the color of the liquid blood a bright vermilion, and when there are no sudden disturbances and only slight variations of level, the Neapolitans are happy. " It is a blessed octave." They think they have evidence that all will go well with them. If, on the contrary, the hard mass does not liquefy at all, or if the liquid blood appear turbid, dark or ash-colored, or if it rises and falls rapidly, or if it presents other unusual and sinister appearances, their hearts sink, and they are filled with alarm and anxiety. They fear that this is an indication of the displeasure of heaven, and that the chastisements they deserve for their sins may soon come on them. We once heard a learned Neapolitan enlarge on this theme, and cite various instances in the history of his city in which he showed a remarkable coincidence, at least, between such facts of the liquefactions and the occurrence of wars, pestilence, famine, and disastrous earthquakes, or of other signal chastisements from heaven. We were not sufficiently conversant with the history of Naples either to controvert his statements or to allege other facts to the contrary. It is a subject on which one might go astray, almost as easily as if he undertook to interpret the Apocalypse. But our friend professed to have the history at his finger-ends, and certainly was himself thoroughly convinced of the truth of his opinion.

Travellers are accustomed to tell amusing stories of the impatience and irreverence of the Neapolitans during the exposition, whenever there is an unusual delay in the liquefaction. They charge them with addressing the saint alternately in expressions of religious homage and of bitter reproach, praying and beseeching him one moment and apostrophizing him the next in slang terms of vituperation. Such travellers, we may be sure, are either drawing on their own imagination or on the store of anecdotes they have heard from others. They usually know little of Italian, and are utterly ignorant of the peculiar dialect of the Neapolitan people—almost a language in itself. The only possible excuse for making such a charge would be a stranger's misconception or misinterpretation of the demonstrative gestures they indulge in when deeply moved, and his utter ignorance of the words they are uttering. We opine, however, that the motive, generally, is a wish to parade droll and amusing statements, even if they be neither witty nor true.

We have been assured by many respectable clergymen of Naples, who, of course, know their own people, and often have to chide them, that there is not a word of truth in this charge.

The clergy and the laity of Naples, of all classes, learned and unlearned alike, believe most steadfastly and earnestly in the miraculous character of the liquefaction of the blood of St. Januarius. Many strangers who have seen it and have examined it critically have come to the same conclusion. Although the church has not spoken authoritatively on the matter, still the consensus of so many learned, intelligent, and pious persons who have so accepted it—the fact that during so many centuries it has stood the test of time, and that science has not been able to explain it away or to reproduce it artificially—and the very character of the liquefaction itself, with its attendant circumstances, so clear, so plain, and so decisive— all leave no room for reasonable doubt.

To complete our statement, we must, perhaps, go still further back, and inquire how it has come about that a portion of the blood of a Christian bishop, beheaded in the year 305, under Diocletian, and in virtue of edicts by that emperor for the suppression of Christianity, should, after the lapse of so many centuries, be now found in a glass ampulla, or vial, at Naples. To some, this primary fact may, at first sight, appear as strange and as extraordinary, if not as unaccountable, as the subsequent liquefaction itself.

To an Italian ·Catholic, indeed, a doubt on this head would scarcely present itself. The usages and the thoughts of his ancestors in the faith have come down to him so naturally that they form, as it were, part of his being. He thinks, and feels, and knows as his fathers did before him. In such cradle-lands of Christianity, and among a people that has never swerved from the faith since the early ages of the church, there is what we might term an inherited Catholic instinct, a readiness and a correctness of Catholic thought in religious matters, which those of other lands that received the light of Christianity only at a later period, and consequently have not such a bond of ancestral connection with the Christians of the days of persecution, can only reach by study and cultivated piety. However, even a moderate acquaintance with the usages and customs of those early ages will show in many instances that what some have considered peculiar national traits of perhaps later growth are in reality deeply rooted in the customs of those ancient times; and that many a point, often set down as a fond fancy or a singular product of superstition, is firmly established as a truth, by historical research into their records.

This is the case with the question before us.

As we study the daily life of those early Christians, passed under circumstances so very different from those of our modern life, and strive to realize to ourselves their thoughts and aspirations, their motives and modes of action, nothing stands out in bolder relief than their exalted conception of the honor and glory of martyrdom. In the exquisite pages of *Fabiola* and of *Callista*, the learned Cardinal Wiseman and Dr. Newman have made these early Christians live again before us; and we catch some insight into their enthusiasm on this subject. To them, a martyr, dying for the faith of Christ, was — and truthfully— a hero of the highest grade. *Greater love than this no man hath, that a man lay down his life for his friends.* John xv. 13.

They could never sufficiently honor him. For, honor him as they might, all they could do would fall infinitely short of the honor which God had already bestowed on his soul in heaven, and that which he would bestow on his body in the resurrection. A martyr's blood, in their view, stood next in rank to the blood of the Saviour.

Their daily life made martyrdom the prominent subject of their thoughts. Day after day, they saw their brethren seized, imprisoned, tortured, and put to death for the faith. Each day, any one of themselves might be seized and led to martyrdom. The greatest of all triumphs, and the surest passport to everlasting bliss, was to persevere unto the end in that conflict ; the greatest of all misfortunes was to fail and renounce or deny the faith for fear of death. Each one strove to hold himself ever ready for the trial. Their pastoral injunctions ; their mutual exhortations; their most precious literature—the *Acta Martyrum ;* the ornamentation of their chapels and crypts, still visible in the frescoes of the catacombs; the site of their chosen sanctuaries, amid the tombs of their martyred brethren; the very altars at which they worshipped; the tombs of their more glorious martyrs—everything co-operated to keep alive this high esteem of martyrdom, and to stir up their hearts to courage, and even to a yearning for so glorious a crown, and so happy an ending of this life of trials and sorrow.

While a confessor of Christ, as they called him, lay still in chains, they used every means to enter the prison and to visit him—sometimes availing themselves of legal rights, sometimes under various pretexts, sometimes by bribery; when these would all fail, then by stealth and at every risk. For he was to be strengthened by the sacraments and encouraged by their words, or they were to be strengthened by his example; and especially they would not lose the opportunity of commending themselves to his prayers, and of seeking the blessing of a chosen friend of God.

When he was led forth to trial, or to torture, or to death, they would glide in among the crowd pressing around him, that he might be cheered and sustained by the sight of Christian faces or by their outspoken exhortations, and that they might catch and embalm in their hearts every courageous word of faith he spoke to his judges, to the executioners, and to themselves or to the crowd, and afterward be able to bear testimony and to record the heroic triumph of another martyr.

After his death, they spared no effort to obtain possession of his mortal remains, as of a most precious treasure. Their very earnestness on this point was not unfrequently made an occasion of aggravating the sentence. After execution, so the judge would order, the body must not be delivered to his friends, according to ordinary usage. These obstinate and fanatical Christians must be thwarted in their dearest wish, or, rather, in their criminal purpose, of honoring one whom the laws had sentenced to an ignominious death. Let the body be burned, and the ashes be cast to the winds or to the running streams; or let the vultures and ravenous dogs consume it; or let it be sunk by weights in deep waters; let it be done away with in some manner, so that the hated Christians be balked of their purpose.

At times this was successfully done. Often, however—even despite these orders—entreaties and bribes to the soldiers and executioners would prevail to obtain the body, or at least the fragments of it. If they failed, stratagems would be used, and persevering search made, even at great personal risk, to recover it. Very often, as the martyrologies and *Acta Martyrum* tell us, it was in such attempts that the Christians were discovered, apprehended, and themselves condemned as fresh victims.

When the execution was by beheading or dismemberment, or such other mode as caused the effusion of blood, the Christians were careful to gather this up in any way they could. Not unfrequently it was all they could recover. Cloths and sponges sucked it up from the hard pavement of wood or stones. The earth saturated with it was carefully gathered up and borne away, that at home and at leisure they might carefully separate the blood from the earthy matter, and place it reverently in some vase, ordinarily of glass, sometimes of earthen ware, and in a few instances of bronze. Sometimes a portion of sponge or of cloth so saturated would be kept as a precious jewel in a locket of silver or gold, and be preserved in the oratory or chapel of a Christian household, or even be reverently borne on the person. Ordinarily, however, the vials or vases into which the martyrs' blood had been gathered, or the open vases containing the saturated sponge or the bundle of blood-stained cloths, would be placed with the body in the tomb; or the vials might be built into the masonry of the tomb, near the head, in such a way as to be partially visible from without.

The *Acta Martyrum*—the official records of the sufferings, death, and deposition or burial of the martyrs, written out at the time by appointed officers of the church—bear frequent testimony to the widespread existence of this custom. Other Christian writings, in prose and in poetry, refer to it frequently. We find it prevailing at Rome and in all Italy, in Carthage, in Sebaste, in Nicomedia, in Gaul, and throughout the church. It was the universal custom.

About the time when the body of St. Januarius was transported from the original tomb where it had been laid during the persecution, to the church of St. Januarius, *extra muros*, at Naples, similar translations of the bodies of martyrs took place elsewhere. St. Ambrose, the great Bishop of Milan, gives an account of such a ceremony for the martyrs St. Gervase and St. Protasius, and again for the martyrs St. Vitalis and St. Agricola. He mentions finding in the tombs, in both cases, the blood of the martyrs which had been gathered and placed there. St. Gaudentius, Bishop of Brixia, about the same time, mentions a similar fact. Some centuries later, the northern barbarians were making raids into Italy, and had repeatedly broken into and desecrated the sepulchres in the catacombs, either in mere wantonness or in search for the treasures which they thought might be hidden there. In order to save the venerated relics of the martyrs from such outrages, the popes opened the tombs of the martyrs in the portions of the catacombs then accessible—a great portion being already closed up, either by the falling in of the roof or by the act of the Christians centuries before—and transferred the remains to the churches within the city for greater safety. In opening the tombs, these vases were often found, and hundreds of them are now in the churches or in the sacred museums of Rome. Three centuries ago, Bosio, and after him Aringhi, Boldetti, Mamachi, and others, penetrated into the catacombs, searched them anew, and came upon some of those portions which had not been disturbed at the time of the general removal. In such portions not a few unopened and undisturbed tombs of martyrs were found. Within lay the remains of the body—bones and dust—with sometimes the rusted fragments of the instrument of death, and frequently the vial, or ampulla, of the martyr's blood. During the last forty years, the work of investigating the catacombs, which had been intermitted, has been taken up afresh and prosecuted with earnestness and skill by F. Marchi, Cav. de Rossi, and other eminent archæologists. They still come occasionally across the tombs of martyrs, evidently untouched since the day of deposition, and within them, or in the mortar by the head, the vases of blood are still found. Where these vials are so placed in the mortar as to be visible and accessible from without, the thin glass has generally been broken. But the bottom still remains firmly set in the mortar, and contains or is covered to some extent by a thin, dry, reddish crust adhering to it. This crust or film is all that is left of the blood the vase originally contained. Vials, or ampullæ, in the interior of the tombs are of course perfectly preserved. It is indeed interesting to look on one of them, and to mark exactly the line to which the liquid blood once reached, and the purple hue of the sediment or crust now left, with its brighter or darker shades of color, perhaps from the character of the blood, more probably from the thickness or thinness of the crust itself. Under all the accumulated evidence, one scarcely needs to read the rude inscription found and still legible, although only scratched in the mortar when it was soft: SANGUIS, or SANG: SATURNINI, *The blood of Saturninus.* We know that this is blood which once flowed from a martyr's veins, in testimony of his faith in Christ our Lord.

In the 17th century, when Bosio, Boldetti, and others brought out such vases from the catacombs, and special attention was directed to them, the nature of this dry reddish crust adhering to the interior was examined chemically. There was no discordance in the results obtained.

Among those who made such an examination was the celebrated Leibnitz, a Protestant, among the ablest and most learned men of that age. He gives an account of his process, and the decision at which he arrived : *This coloring matter on the glass is sanguineous.* Some years ago, the present Pontiff, Pius IX., had a new analysis made according to the fullest and most accurate tests of modern chemistry. The answer was still the same : This substance is, so far as chemistry can decide, precisely what

ought to remain as the residuum of human blood.

It is clear that, both as to the custom of the early Christians of carefully gathering up the blood of their martyrs, of placing it in ampullæ, or vases, and religiously preserving it, and likewise as to the identification of the ampullæ themselves, the testimony is all that can be desired. Bosio, Aringhi, Boldetti, Mamachi, Gaume, Marchi, Raoul-Rochette, De Rossi, Perret—all who have studied the question, are unanimous in recognizing these numerous old Roman vials, or ampullæ, still found in the catacombs and tombs or preserved in the churches, as the identical vials, or ampullæ, so used by the ancient Christians. On this point, there remains not the slightest room for doubt.

It is therefore but reasonable that there should exist in Naples a vial, or ampulla, of the blood of St. Januarius. He was in his day a distinguished bishop of the church. His martyrdom was public, and attracted the attention of the Christians. It was by beheading. There was no conceivable reason why the Christians should omit in that instance what they were universally so careful to do in such cases. On the contrary, to judge from the ancient accounts we have of the martyrdom of St. Januarius and his six companions, the Christians found no extraordinary difficulty in obtaining the bodies, and entombing them in their usual mode. When, eighty or ninety years later, the church had been firmly established in peace, the body of St. Januarius was taken from the original tomb and brought to Naples, as the bodies of the others were taken to the various churches which claimed them.

The very presence, tnerefore, of an ampulla in the custody of the church of Naples, together with the other relics of St. Januarius, is under the circumstances *prima facie* evidence of its own authenticity—evidence which cannot be impugned, except by attempting to overturn a well-known and universally admitted usage of the early Christian church, or else by a supposition, equally gratuitous and absurd, that the ampulla which originally was in existence, and was prized beyond measure and carefully preserved, was somehow lost, and another fraudulently substituted in its stead. We need not recur to the olden traditions of the church of Naples or its legends concerning this relic—traditions and legends found, too, we believe, among the Greeks, whose intercourse with Magna Grecia, as Southern Italy was called, was more intimate and continued longer than with any other portion of Italy. We scarcely need the testimony of *Fabius Jordanus*, quoted by Caraccioli, going to show that, so far back as A.D. 685, it was the custom of the clergy of Naples to bear the relics of the head.

The historical evidence in favor of the genuineness of the relic is ample and satisfactory. There would not be a moment's hesitation on the point but for the very vain hope which some minds may entertain that, by declining to admit the genuineness of the blood, they will somehow escape the difficulties of the liquefaction. As if the liquefaction of any other substance, with all the circumstances which characterize the liquefaction at Naples, as we have set them forth in our previous articles, would not be for them as hard if not a harder nut to crack than the liquefaction of the blood of St. Januarius!

Having, therefore, established the genuineness of the relic, the next question which presents itself is this: Are we to attribute the amount of the blood still to be seen within the ampulla when at its ordinary level, and its condition when hard, to the continuous action of natural causes; or are we to recognize in those points the effects of that supernatural force to which the liquefaction itself is to be attributed? Would or would not the agency of natural causes have resulted in a greater reduction of the original volume of the blood, and in a far different condition of the residuum, at the present time?

We know pretty accurately the composition of human blood. The proportions of the several ingredients going to constitute it may vary somewhat according to the health and the food of individuals. Without entering into the refined, and as yet not fully accepted results of the latest qualitative analysis, it will be sufficient to give the following table of the constituents of the healthy blood of man:

Water,		790·37	
Albumen,		67·80	
Oxygen,			
Nitrogen,			serum,
Carbonic acid,			869·7,5
Extractive matters,		10·98	
Salts,			
Coloring matter,			
Fibrine,		2·95	
Hæmatine,	2·27		clot,
Globuline,	125·63		130·8,5
Blood globules,		127·90	
		1,000·00	1,000·00

Water constitutes nearly four-fifths of the entire quantity. If it be driven off by evaporation, only a dry mass would remain behind.

When blood issues from the veins, it first passes through the process of coagulation, the successive steps of which have been carefully examined. Perfectly liquid as it comes out, the blood soon thickens, through the action of the fibrine it contains, into a firm, elastic, uniform, jelly-like mass. Soon drops of clear, amber-colored fluid begin to exude from the mass of jelly, and accumulate until the whole mass is divided into two parts—the serum, a transparent, nearly colorless fluid, in which there floats the clot, or crassamentum, a firm, red and opaque mass. In time, the clot is further divided. The fibrine is seen at top, forming a layer of considerable consistence, soft, elastic, tenacious, and of a yellowish white color; the under portion, consisting of the heavier parts of the clot which have gradually settled down to that position, is a red mass, made up chiefly of the blood globules.

Further exposure would by degrees eliminate the aqueous portion by evaporation, and the progress of decomposition would tend to free the gases in the other constituents, and thus still further to diminish the mass. But no experiments, instituted by physicists, can compare, in time at least, with the instances presented to us in the vases of the catacombs. There, traces on the glass still show clearly to what level the blood, or at least the clot, originally reached; and we see what has remained after a lapse of sixteen hundred years—a crust of dry reddish powder adhering to and coating the sides and bottom of the vessel.

Boldetti, however, mentions three instances in which such ampullæ were found in the catacombs containing a residuum of the blood still thick and slightly liquid. And, if we are not mistaken, something similar may be seen in some other vials preserved here and there, and held to contain a portion of the blood of certain martyrs.

The early Christians of Italy gave up the old Roman custom of incremation, or burning the bodies of the dead, and adopted instead the Eastern rite of sepulture. In some instances, at least, they seem to have used spices and ointments, as the Jews and Eastern nations generally did; and some of them might even have had a knowledge of the antiseptic preparations used by the Egyptians. They never prepared the dead as mummies, but they may at times have put some antiseptic ingredient into the blood, tending by its chemical action somehow to retard the escape of the water and the decomposition of the mass. If this were really done or not, we believe modern science cannot decide; and the historical evidence is not clear.

Something may be due, also, to the mode in which they would sometimes close a narrow-necked vessel of glass. When it had received its contents, the glass of the neck would be heated, probably by the flame of a blowpipe, until it became soft and pliable. The sides would then be pressed together until they coalesced and became united, thus obliterating the orifice; or else molten glass would be carefully dropped on the lips of the mouth, until the whole was entirely coated over and perfectly closed. When either was followed and the work was done perfectly, the ampulla would be, in fact, hermetically sealed. The air would thus be excluded, and evaporation nearly arrested. Placed in a *loculus* or grave in the dry earth of the catacombs, twenty-five or thirty-five feet beneath the surface of the earth, the ampulla would also be subjected to an ever-equable temperature of about 58° Fahr. Under such circumstances, especially if we admit the presence of some antiseptic ingredient, it may be possible that decomposition would be very slow. But, after all, the glass sides of these ampullæ are thin, and glass is porous, and sixteen centuries is a very long time. Even were the sides far thicker than they are, evaporation would have slowly taken place, the gaseous products of decomposition would have gradually passed through into the outer atmosphere, and only the dry solid residuum would be left, as we ordinarily find it in the ampullæ from the catacombs. The case of the ampulla containing the blood of St. Januarius is not open to these doubts. We are not able to say, indeed, whether it was actually closed in either of the modes we have indicated. As it stands in the present reliquary, of which we have given an account, the mouth enters so deeply into the upper mass of soldering within the case that the eye cannot discover the manner of closure. Before it was placed in this reliquary, five hundred and seventy or seven hundred and thirty years ago, this could probably have been seen; but we have found no record throwing light on the subject. We presume it was done in one or the other of the modes we have described. It is certainly so tightly closed that not a drop of the liquid blood within has ever been known to ooze out.

But this ampulla has not been lying in the low and equable temperature of an underground vault of the catacombs. It has been preserved in the upper and variable atmosphere of a city, subject for many centuries to the excessive heats of almost tropical summers, and to the cold winds that blow down at times from mountains covered with snow. By no law of physics could a mass of blood so

situated escape the natural consequence—a vast diminution of bulk by the loss of water and the escape of gases. The film that coats the interior of the smaller ampulla seen in the same case or reliquary, so like the film seen in the whole and in the broken ampullæ of the catacombs and churches generally, shows, we think, what would have been the natural course.

That the larger ampulla should, on the contrary, have lost nothing in the volume of its contents—that it should still be four-fifths filled, although for centuries exposed, as we have said, to heat and cold—that this general permanence of bulk and of character should be maintained, although eighteen or twenty times a year the mass alternates from a solid to a fluid condition, and passes through many subordinate changes of color and volume—these facts seem to us not only utterly inexplicable, but directly contrary to all we know of physical laws. We place them along side the grand fact of the liquefaction itself, as being in some measure its characteristic concomitants. Still, should any one deem these questions too obscure to be peremptorily decided, we shall not now discuss them. We are quite willing to let them stand or fall with the more prominent and important and more tangible question of the liquefaction itself. Of that we shall now proceed to treat.

IV.

AFTER the very full and detailed exposition of the facts of the liquefactions, as millions have seen them in the past—as tens of thousands may, and do still, see them each year—the question forces itself on us: Is this a miracle, as the Neapolitans believe, and as many earnest and critical examiners from other lands have been led to hold, after a careful and candid investigation into the facts of the case? Is it a suspension of the ordinary laws of nature, and an intervention of the supernatural power of the Most High, producing an effect above and beyond the ordinary course of nature? or is this liquefaction a phenomenon entirely within the sphere of natural laws—either the result of some law, or combination of laws, producing this effect; or is it the result of the art and skill of men? One of these three it must be: either the spontaneous effect of some natural laws, or the artificial result of human trickery, or a miracle. The decision must depend on the character of the facts.

The Neapolitans, and, with them, Catholic writers generally, hold it to be a miracle. On the other hand, such a visible substantiation of the claims made by the Catholic Church that miracles do continue in her fold, as the Saviour promised, and are the seal and confirmation of her divine authority, has not failed to arouse the opposition of those who deny that authority.

In meeting the argument, or the facts of the case, they have not always followed the same line. Two or three centuries ago, they contended that the liquefaction was a lying wonder produced by witchcraft or magic, or by the power of Beelzebub. A little later, natural philosophy was appealed to. This liquefaction of the blood, when the vial was brought near to the head, arose, they said, from a law of sympathy in nature, akin to if not merely a peculiar form of that law which causes blood to flow from the wounds of a corpse if the real murderer lay his hand on the dead body.

These replies, or attempts at a natural solution, are antiquated. We need not seriously consider them.

In the last century, the objectors took a very different ground. The whole thing, they said, was a device of the priests. Some called it a "trick of long standing and great ingenuity"; others stigmatized it as "one of the most bungling tricks ever seen." This style of objection still holds its own.

During the present century, another style of objection has come into vogue, based on the ever-increasing spirit of rationalism. The laws of nature, we are told, are invariable and supreme. No violations of them are possible. All miracles—in the sense of occurrences above and beyond those laws of nature, occasional interruptions in the grand scheme of universal order, law, and causation—are to be at once rejected. "The idea of *their* possibility can only occur to those who have failed to grasp the great inductive principle of invariable uniformity and law in nature." "It is hardly a question of evidence. The generality of mankind habitually assume antecedently that miracles are now inadmissible; and hence, that, in any reported case, they must in some manner be explained away. . . . Of old, the sceptic professed he would be convinced by seeing a miracle. At the present day, a visible miracle would be the very subject of his scepticism. It is not the attestation, but the nature of the alleged miracle, which is now the point in question. It is not the fallibility of human testimony, but the infallibility of natural order, which is now the ground of argument." (Rev. Baden Powell, *Order of Nature.*)

We have not the space to examine this theory at length, and to show that it is at bottom anti-christian and pantheistic, contrary to the soundest principles of true philosophy. Nor is it necessary for our purpose to do so. All the philosophical disquisitions in the world will not prove to a man having eyes that, because "the laws of nature are immutable, and miracles `are therefore impossible," the blood which stands in the ampulla was liquid when taken out, or is solid at the conclusion. He saw that it was hard, and sees that it is now fluid. He will laugh at the philosopher and believe his own eyes.

Neither is it necessary to confute at length the opinion accepted so blindly by Protestants, that the age of miracles has long since past, and that miracles have entirely ceased since the days of the apostles. If God can work miracles, what man can limit him in the exercise of that power, either in time or place? And did not the Saviour promise the continuance of signs among them that believe—a continuance to which he put no limitation?

The assertion that the Catholic Church is erroneous, and that consequently there can be no miracles in her fold, is more than akin to the words of the Pharisees to the blind man whom our Lord had restored to sight: "*Give glory to God; we know that this man is a sinner.*" The appropriate answer was: "*If he be a sinner, I know not: one thing I know, that whereas I was blind, now I see*" (John ix. 24, 25).

We therefore leave the general subject of miracles to be treated by others; and we confine ourselves to the fact of the liquefaction. In this, as in every other case of alleged miracles, the decision depends entirely on the character of the testimony and on the nature of the facts which that testimony establishes.

The testimony in this case is overwhelming in amount and unimpeachable in character. The liquefaction with its marked features and details are clearly established. We have only to seek its cause.

Is it due to the regular action of the natural laws which, under the given circumstances, produce the liquefaction, independently of any special act of men designed to bring it about? How does a solid body naturally pass into a fluid condition?

A solid body may become fluid by deliquescence. Certain substances drink in water from the atmosphere around them to such an extent as to become fluid. They are said to deliquesce.

Is this liquefaction a deliquescence? Most assuredly not.

1. The substance within the ampulla—the indurated blood—so far as the eye can judge of it, through the glass of the ampulla and the glass sides of the reliquary, bears no resemblance to any of the substances which are known to deliquesce.

2. The process of deliquescence is well known and is not to be mistaken. It is gradual; and the exterior of the deliquescing substance, being in immediate contact with the water-bearing atmosphere, is always seen to yield first to the liquefying influence of the water. On the contrary, the liquefaction is often instantaneous—*in un colpo d'occhio ; in un tratto.* Even when gradual and not instantaneous, the differences are marked. The upper portion will become perfectly liquid while the lower portion remains still hard; or the lower portion will liquefy while the upper portion retains its hardness; or, again, the upper and lower portions may both remain hard while the middle portion becomes fluid ; or the middle portion will continue hard and solid while they become perfectly liquid : sometimes, the outer surface next to the glass sides of the ampulla will be seen to soften and liquefy first—in this case following the course of a deliquescence; sometimes precisely the reverse occurs—the central portion is seen to become liquid while the exterior remains hard and unliquefied. When we add that occasionally one side or lateral half liquefies while the other preserves its hardness, and also that, while frequently the entire mass becomes liquid, yet, on many occasions, a certain portion remains hard for hours and days and then liquefies—perhaps gradually, perhaps only after the entire mass has become hardened again —it will be seen that this liquefaction presents every possible mode and shade of difference to distinguish it from the single mode of deliquescence.

The difficulty becomes greater if we consider the obstacles to a freer communication between the outer atmosphere and the substance within the ampulla. The ampulla is a tightly-closed glass vessel, and is itself held within the reliquary, another tightly-closed vessel of metal and glass. This twofold barrier must forbid any ready and rapid passage of atmospheric water from the air to the substance within the ampulla.

Again, no connection whatever can be discovered between the superabundant moisture or the dryness of the atmosphere at Naples and the occurrence or non-occurrence of the liquefaction. We may take a series of twenty days, which the diary marks as very rainy, or occurring in a long-continued rainy season ; and a series of twenty others, when the weather was dry—so dry, they were praying for rain. It will be seen that the phases of the liquefactions for each series are so alike that they might be interchanged. The general hygrometric condition of the atmosphere evidently has no perceptible influence for or against or on the liquefactions.

Nay, more, it frequently happens that the blood, after liquefying, grows solid again on the same day, and then liquifies, perhaps solidifies anew, and liquefies a third time. All these changes have sometimes taken place within one hour. Now, did the atmosphere, during that hour or during that day, pass through corresponding extreme changes of its hygrometric condition? Ordinary men did not feel them. Meteorological observers have not noticed them. Registering instruments do not record them. And yet, the habit of watching their neighboring and often threatening volcano has made the people of Naples as observant of such changes as sailors at sea, and has given to that city one of the ablest schools of meteorology on the Continent.

We may well conclude, therefore, that the liquefaction of the blood of St. Januarius is not the deliquescence of a solid body, arising from humidity of the air to which it is exposed.

Is it the melting of a solid substance through the action of heat?

This is a more important question. Many of those who charge bad faith and trickery on the "priests and monks" officiating at the expositions, maintain that it is by an adroit application of heat that the liquefaction is brought about. Others, who admit the sincerity and good faith of the Neapolitan clergy—which, knowing the men, they feel cannot be impugned—still attribute the liquefaction to the heat of the altar, all ablaze with lighted tapers, and of the crowd thronging the chapel, and packed most closely just in the sanctuary itself and around the altar.

We undertake to show that the liquefaction is in no way produced by or dependent on heat.

I. Often, when the crowd is greatest, and the heat most intense—say in September—the liquefaction is delayed for hours; perhaps does not occur at all, or only a portion liquefies, while another portion remains solid.

II. On the contrary, it has occurred quickly and for the entire mass, even though the crowd was comparatively small. This is especially seen in the extraordinary expositions, even in winter, when not a score of persons were present.

III. It has taken place in the open air, while the reliquary, placed upright in an open framework, and held aloft above the heads of the people, was borne in procession through the streets; and this in the winter months of December and January, as well as on the vigils at the beginning of May.

IV. It has occurred on days when snow covered the streets, or the cold was so excessive as to cause the usual procession through the streets to be dispensed with. As the churches in Naples are not heated, the temperature within the cathedral must have been very low, probably not above 45° Fahrenheit.

V. This very question has been submitted to scientific investigation. The professors of the Royal University of Naples, headed by Dr. *Nicholas Fergola*, the most eminent physicist of the faculty, instituted a number of interesting observations, which Dr. Fergola published. We copy from his work a table giving the actual temperature in a number of instances, as shown by a standard thermometer which they stationed on the altar in close proximity to the reliquary at the time of the liquefaction:

TABLE.

OBSERVATIONS FOR TEMPERATURE AND TIME AND CHARACTER OF THE LIQUEFACTION
OF THE BLOOD OF ST. JANUARIUS, MADE BY THE PROFESSORS OF THE ROYAL
UNIVERSITY, NAPLES.

A, date ; B, temperature, *Fahr.*; C, number of minutes which elapsed from the commencement of the exposition of the relics on the altar, until the liquefaction of the blood ; D, character of the liquefaction.

A.		B.	C.	D.
1794. Sept. 19......		80°	27′	From hard to perfectly liquid.
	20......	80	21	" " " liquid.
	21......	80	19	" " " "
	22......	78	24	" " " "
	23......	77	25	" " " "
	24......	78	5	" " " "
	25......	80	10	" " " "
	26......	77	5	" " " "
1795. May. 2......		76	12	" " " semi-liquid.
	3......	76	2	" " " perfectly liquid.
	4......	77	41	" " " liquid.*
	5......	80	22	" " " " *
	6......	75	12	" " " " *
	7......	76	29	" " " " *
	8......	77	29	" " " " *
	9......	80	33	" " " " *
	10......	67	15	" " " "
1795. Sept. 19......		74	25	" " " " with floating lump.
	20......	78	26	" " " perfectly liquid.
	21......	81	27	" " " " "
	22......	78	25	" " " " "
	23......	80	24	" " " " "
	24......	81	32	" " " " "
	25......	78	18	" " " " "
	26......	74	3	" " " " "

On the six days in May, marked *, the reliquary was placed on its stand on the altar about mid-day, for the afternoon intermissions. A silk veil was thrown over it ; and it was left undisturbed until after 3 P.M. At that hour, the blood was found hard each day ; and subsequently it liquefied again, during the afternoon service.

The foregoing very important table speaks for itself. Once the temperature stood at 67°, and the liquefaction took place in 15 minutes, although the day before, with the thermometer standing at 80°, it had been delayed more than twice that time. Twice the thermometer marked 74° ; the liquefaction was delayed in one instance only 3 minutes ; in the other, full 25 minutes. Once the temperature was 75°. In that case 12 minutes of delay were counted. Thrice it was 76° ; and the times were 2 minutes, 12 minutes, and 29 minutes. Four times it was 77° ; the liquefaction occurred after a lapse of 5, 25, 29, and 41 minutes, respectively. Five times the thermometer stood at 78° ; and the times of delay in the several cases were 5, 18, 24, 25, and 26 minutes. Seven times it stood at 80° ; and the delays were respectively 10, 19, 21, 22, 24, 27, and 33 minutes. The highest point observed at the time of the liquefaction was 81°. It was reached twice. Here again the times differed. On one occasion the liquefaction was delayed 27 minutes ; on the other, 32 minutes.

In view of these varied results from so many careful tests, the commission of professors could only report, as they did, and as Dr. Fergola maintains in his essay, that the liquefaction of the blood of St. Januarius evidently does not depend on the degree of heat to which it is subjected during the expositions.

VI. The same conclusion may also be reached by a single consideration. When a solid substance is liquefied or melted by heat, it will continue liquid if the heat is kept at the same temperature or rises. It will resume its solid condition only when the temperature falls below that degree which is the melting point of the substance.

Now, in those summer days which we have spoken of—such as the six days of May, 1795, marked in the table of Fergola—days on which the Neapolitans seek the repose of a *siesta* — the hottest hours are from 12 M. to 3 P.M. During these hours, the temperature is naturally higher than it was at 9.30 or 10 A.M., or is afterward at 4 P.M., or later. Yet the blood, which liquefied at 9.30 or 10 A.M., almost invariably becomes solid again during these hottest hours, if the reliquary be placed on the altar and a silk veil thrown over it, and it liquefies again during the afternoon exposition, although the heat of the day is then sensibly diminishing.

The more accurately and carefully the facts of the liquefaction are studied, the more clearly do we see that it does not depend on temperature, general or local. It is not produced by the action of heat.

This exclusion of the agency of heat has " considerably exercised " some of the opponents of the liquefaction of the blood of St. Januarius. Confident that all miracles are, now at least, inadmissible, and that this and every other alleged miracle is susceptible of a natural explanation, if we only knew it, they eagerly

catch at any, even the most far-fetched and improbable theories, and put them forward with equal inconsiderateness and confidence.

We have heard it said : Oh ! Naples is an exceptional, volcanic district. There may exist there some occult or obscure volcanic agency, which suffices to produce the liquefaction; who can tell what strange results may come from a combination of all the volcanic agencies ever at work in that vicinity ?

Is Naples the only volcanic district in the world ? Does any other volcanic district present anything like this liquefaction, or calculated to throw light on it ? Even in Naples, is there another similar example ? And has not this liquefaction continued regularly, even when Vesuvius was quiescent for a long term of years. Previous to December, 1631, the volcano had slumbered in perfect tranquillity for nearly two centuries. A French traveller tells of the flocks of cattle he saw browsing within the very crater itself, then a vast green valley sunk in the plateau forming the top of the mountain. Yet all this while the liquefactions continued as they had done before, and as they have done ever since, in other seasons of quiet, and in seasons of active volcanic eruption.

And then, we ask, what other sign or indication is there giving evidence of this natural influence or law ? And what sort of a natural law is that which acts only on one single vial of blood, and has not acted on the thousands of others in the same conditions.

Again, it has been urged, in much the same strain, that our knowledge of the laws of nature is still very imperfect. Many laws are as yet undiscovered. Every year is marked by some advance in our knowledge of them. It by no means follows that this liquefaction is miraculous, merely because as yet we are unable to assign the precise law or laws of nature which govern it. Perhaps, some time, men will discover them. Then all will be plain. Until then, they tell us, philosophy requires us to note carefully and accurately the facts of the case, and to wait for some explanation or solution of them in the future.

It is always well to take note of the facts, and to make our theories subordinate to those facts. What we find fault with our opponents for, in this question, is that they do precisely the reverse: they fix a theory in their minds, and if the facts of the case do not agree with their theory, why, so much the worse for the facts.

One word on the laws of nature. Although there may be many of which we have now no knowledge, and which we may hereafter discover, still we do know some. These may be supplemented—they cannot be contradicted or reversed by any laws hereafter to be discovered. The legitimate conclusions based on the certain knowledge which we have, are not to be impugned or held doubtful until we discover other laws. We do know, for example, that when a man's head is severed from his body, he dies. All the known and unknown laws of nature cannot make him live again.

It will not do to base an argument in one paragraph on the invariable uniformity of law and order in nature, and, in the next, to maintain that we are as yet all at sea about these laws.

Among the well-known and uncontested laws of nature by which we may be guided in our argument, are several which have a close connection with the subject before us. We refer to them.

I. We know that solid bodies become liquid by increase of temperature; for each body, there is a certain melting-point. Above that, the solid body becomes liquid; below that, it remains solid, or returns to solidity.

II. The same liquid, at the same temperature, has the same volume, or occupies the same space. It is on this law that our thermometers are constructed.

These two laws are known and established beyond doubt, if anything is known or established beyond doubt in physical science. Let us consider them in reference to the substance which is seen to liquefy in the vial or ampulla in the reliquary.

I. This substance has no fixed melting-point. Looking at Fergola's table, we see that it liquefied one day at 67° in 15 minutes, while the day before, at 80°, it liquefied only in 33 minutes. One day at 76° it liquefied perfectly in 2 minutes, and the next day at 77° it occupied 41 minutes. It has liquefied in the month of January, during a procession in the public street, while it was borne aloft on a stand, and freely exposed to the general temperature —then probably between 50° and 60°, if not lower. At other times, in midsummer, with a temperature over 80°, it has remained solid and unliquefied for hours and for days. Nay, after having become liquid, it frequently solidifies again, just at the hours between 12 M. to 3 P.M., when the heat of the day reaches its maximum. It is clear that this liquefaction completely sets aside the first-mentioned law of the melting-point.

II. The law of volume is set aside with equal peremptoriness. As you look at the liquid in the vial, you see that it changes in volume, either increasing or decreasing. Sometimes the liquid occupies only about three-fourths of the space within the vial. Before your eyes, it will increase, sometimes with froth, sometimes even bubbling more or less violently, sometimes retaining a perfectly tranquil and level surface; sometimes rising very slowly, sometimes rapidly; and it may continue to rise until it fills the vial. Or again, if the vial be full, or nearly full, the liquid within it will sink, either suddenly or gradually, hour by hour, with or without froth or bubbling, until it occupies perhaps three-fourths of the space. These changes take place in summer and in winter indifferently. They are entirely independent of the temperature. They evidently set aside the second law we have recited regarding volume.

III. A third law of nature is, that her steps are forward and not backward. A movement once made is never revoked. Chemical changes are progressive, and, so long as the ingredients and agents remain the same, they never go back to repeat a combination which has once been made and then changed for another.

Yet continual repetitions of the same forms, combinations, or conditions of the substance within the ampulla are a special characteristic of the liquefactions.

We will produce, hereafter, in a fitting place, evidence that for centuries the ampulla has not been opened, and consequently that its contents have not been changed. Nevertheless, the alternate hardenings and liquefactions, the variations of color, the frothing, and the ebullitions, and the increases and decreases of volume, have continued to succeed each other, and to be repeated hundreds, some of them thousands, of times.

Nay, leaving aside for the moment these longer periods, and confining our examination to the ten or twelve hours of a single day, during which

the ampulla is all the while under the public gaze, and any interference of chemical art with the contents is absolutely impossible, we still find these repetitions of the same form or combination. The blood was solid when first taken out, it liquefied, stood liquid for an hour or two, solidified again, and again liquefied. Perhaps it solidified a third time, and a third time liquefied. It commenced to froth, and it ceased, then commenced again, and again ceased. It changed color, and again returned to the prestine tint. It changed in bulk, either increasing or decreasing, and again returned to its former level.

This reiteration of some or of all of these changes, in a single day, while the ingredients in the ampulla are evidently neither added to nor diminished, is contrary to the course of nature. The opposition is seen, the same in character, but manifested in vaster proportions, when evidence compels us to admit that the substance in the ampulla has not been changed or meddled with for years, and even for centuries; while yet these reiterations ever continue. The argument is the same in both instances.

There is no uncertainty as to the facts of the liquefaction or the well-known laws of nature which we have referred to. Nor is there any doubt that the facts are violations of those laws. Other laws of nature, yet to be discovered, may fill gaps in our knowledge, and may complement the laws already known. None will be discovered to contradict or upset them. It is as vain to wait for the discovery of some unknown law which may account for the facts of the liquefaction, as it would be to look for some other unknown law of nature in virtue of which Lazarus lived again, and came forth from the tomb—a law which, curiously enough, happened to act just at the moment when our Saviour stood before the tomb, and cried out: " *Lazarus, come orth.*"

Can anything be more absurd than this theory which, with words of seeming scientific ⁻caution and of wide philosophic views, would attribute the liquefaction to the action of some as yet undiscovered laws. In truth, what sort of a regular natural law would that be which manifests its unshakable uniformity by somehow or other coming into play, and producing the liquefaction, just at those precise days, hours, and places which men have from time to time selected, because convenient to them or suited to their thoughts of religion—a law which caused the blood to liquefy regularly on the 14th of January, each year, so long as that day was celebrated as a festival; and skipped back to December 16 when a new festival on that day was substituted instead—which is ready to put off the liquefaction from the 16th of December to the Sunday following, whether the delay be of one, two, three, four, five, or six days, according to the day of the week on which the 16th may fall, and continues its complaisant action for the quarter of a century during which several archbishops of Naples preferred a celebration on the Sunday after to a celebration on the 16th of December itself; and which was quite ready to go back again to liquefying the blood on the 16th of December as soon as another archbishop decided to return to the old usage—which is equally accommodating in May, and always commences its series of liquefactions for nine consecutive days precisely on the Saturday before the first Sunday in May, regardless of whether it fell on April 30 or any day after up to and including May 6—and which, stranger yet, has been known often to adapt itself to the journeyings of strangers coming to Naples, and to bring into play its power of liquefaction on the very days and hours when these strangers could come to the *tesoro* chapel, and the ecclesiastical and the civil authorities had come to an understanding, and the relics were brought out and placed on the altar?

It is useless to multiply words. The theory of general law must be ruled out, as utterly inconsistent with the facts of the case.

Whenever the liquefaction occurs, it must be each time in consequence of something done or occurring on that occasion; either because of something done by man intentionally and advisedly for the express purpose of producing the liquefaction, or perchance unintentionally—that is, without a knowledge of the effect to follow—or else because of the exercise on the part of God of his supernatural power, in answer to the faith and earnest prayers of a believing people. In this case, it is a miracle, as the Neapolitans and those who agree with them steadfastly hold it to be.

We have already stated facts amply sufficient to exclude one arm of this alternative. The liquefaction cannot be the natural result of any action of man, whether intentional or accidental. Any liquefaction produced by the art of man would of course be within the sphere of natural action, and would necessarily be subject to the natural laws of liquefaction. If produced by heat, the law of the melting-point would be observed. If it in any way depended on the mutual action of chemical ingredients, the laws of such action would never be seen to be reversed and set aside repeatedly, even in a single day. ᵀn whatever way the liquid was obtained, it would observe the law of constant volume at the same temperature, and would not so frequently either decrease or increase its bulk. In one word, man has no power to set aside the laws of nature as we plainly see them set aside in this liquefaction. We are forced to conclude that it is not his work. The liquefaction which is seen at Naples is not, and cannot possibly be, the natural result of any art or skill, or of any blundering of the Neapolitan clergy.

This will be made still clearer if circumstances allow us to examine somewhat in detail, as we hope to do in a closing article, the various solutions which have been proposed, and the attempted imitations of this liquefaction. Their signal failure in every instance serves as practical confirmations of the conclusion to which we have been already led. If with the aids of science and skill at their command, men have failed to reproduce the liquefaction of the blood of St. Januarius, is it not clear that the priests and monks of Naples are not competent of themselves to produce the original?

The liquefaction must be, as the Neapolitans hold it to be, a *miracle* —a fact contrary to the laws of nature, wrought by the power of God for a purpose worthy of himself.

V.

THE direct and positive arguments which we have presented in our last article, bearing on the miraculous character of the liquefaction, cover the ground so entirely that we might, indeed, rest our case on their presentation. We need, however, make no apology for going further, and examining also, and somewhat in detail, the difficulties and counter-statements which have been made, from time to time, by those who deny its miraculous character. Truth shrinks from no examination or proper test. .

We are confident that, the more closely those objections are examined, the weaker they will be found to be; and their weakness is an additional argument for the truth of our conclusion.

The general charge is that this liquefaction is effected by some trick or other on the part of the priests. A vague charge by itself means nothing, and is of no value. To be worth anything, there must follow a "specification," some indication or explanation of the precise mode or trick by which the liquefaction is effected. HOW IS IT DONE? This is the first question to which a reply must be given, before the objectors can come into court.

The replies to it have been numerous, very numerous—in fact, so numerous as to lose all real value: they are so wonderfully discordant and so contradictory.

The liquefaction of the blood of St. Januarius has occurred, during the last two hundred and fifty years —to go no further back just now—at least four thousand times; in public, without any attempt at concealment, under the eyes of believers and unbelievers alike, standing on every side and within a few feet, it may be, in immediate contact with the officiating clergyman, and, therefore, possessing ample opportunity for the closest and most critical inspection of everything concerning it. Under such circumstances, it is inconceivable that the precise trick, or fraud, or secret, if there were any, should remain undiscovered. Yet, that no such discovery has been made is perfectly clear from this striking disagreement among those who charge that there is fraud, as soon as they undertake to state distinctly in what the fraud or trick consists. What one proposes is scouted by another as so weak and so contrary to the facts of the case, that it is virtually a surrender of the cause. One declares it to be "one of the most bungling tricks he ever saw"; but he is entirely silent as to the nature of the trick so obvious to him. Another states it to be a trick "of great ingenuity," as well as of "long standing"; but, with equal prudence, he also is mute as to its character. A third will explain the manner in which A. thought it was done; and the very different manner in which B. held that it was performed; while C. with equal shrewdness proposed a third mode. The reader is considerably left free to select which he pleases. Which of them or whether any one of them be actually true is apparently a question of minor importance. The grand purpose aimed at—and for that, any one of them, even if a mistake, will, it is thought, be sufficient—is to find some passable or colorable pretext to relieve the reader from the exceedingly disagreeable necessity of admitting a popish miracle.

When two and a half centuries of keen and critical examinations, covering so many thousand instances of the liquefaction, have resulted only in such utter confusion and disagreement among those who profess to have discovered the fraud, we may legitimately conclude that in reality there has been no discovery of any trickery or fraud whatsoever.

Not to tax the reader's patience too much, we will endeavor to classify the various modes in which we are assured by these discordant voices that the fraud is perpetrated.

The first class attributes the liquefaction, or seeming liquefaction, to some kind of jugglery or *legerdemain* practised by the officiating clergymen during the exposition of the relics.

But *when*, or *how*, it would puzzle Houdin himself, or the Fakir of Ava, to say.

Is it, as some have suggested, the adroit substitution of a second reliquary which contains a liquid, and which, at a suitable moment, is presented to the bystanders, instead of the original reliquary containing a hard substance?

Most certainly not. The officiating priest stands in front of an altar built of marble and bronze, without drawers or hiding-places. The reliquary in his hands is of considerable bulk—twelve inches high, five inches broad, and two and a half or three inches thick—entirely too large to elude the keen eyesight of the hundreds close around, who intently watch it and scan every motion of the clergyman. Where could the second reliquary lie hidden until needed? Could he lay down the first one and hide it away, and draw forth the second one and exhibit it to the people, without some such movement of his hands and arms as must inevitably be seen? Can it be that never once in these four thousand times did any eye detect the act of substitution? Many of the chaplains and canons who officiate are aged men. Can their feeble or half-paralyzed arms do frequently, regularly, and always with perfect success, what the most expert and practised prestigitator would shrink from attempting? The thing is utterly impossible.

If it were possible and actually done, it would not answer the requirements of the case. In such a substitution, the liquefaction would *always* appear to be instantaneous—as instantaneous as the adroit substitution. But the real process of liquefaction is seldom so instantaneous. It is often gradual, occupying an appreciable, sometimes a long time. It may often be followed by the eye in the various stages from solidity to perfect fluidity.

Moreover, no substitution can account for the subsequent hardenings, or the alternations of hardenings and liquefactions, especially when these occur, as they sometimes do, while the reliquary remains untouched, mounted on its stand on the altar, in the sight of all, or during a procession in the streets when it is borne aloft, equally untouched, in its open frame, and is equally visible to all.

The idea of a substitution of reliquaries can only be entertained by one who is utterly ignorant of the circumstances of the liquefaction.

We set it aside. If nothing else can be said, the miracle must stand.

The publicity of all the movements of the officiating clergyman who holds the reliquary, and the unceasing inspection of the reliquary by so many observers on every side, are equally peremptory in excluding the supposition that the liquefaction may possibly be produced by inserting, during the exposition, some new ingredient into the ampulla, which, uniting with the hard substance already there, will give a third substance of a liquid character. How could this be done so many thousand times and always under the eyes of a crowd of most attentive and watchful observers, without a single one of them ever, in a single instance, detecting this new substance while held in reserve for the proper moment, or noticing the act of inserting it, as this precedes the liquefaction? And what shall we say of those numerous cases in which the blood, having liquefied, becomes hard again, and, after a time, liquefies again? Is there an adroit withdrawal of this new ingredient from the ampulla in order that the liquid may harden again, and is there a fresh application of it, each time, for every renewal of the liquefaction, during the day? And what if these changes occur while the reliquary is not in the hands of the clergyman at all, but has been placed and remains all the while on its stand on the altar, or is borne aloft in its open frame during a procession? Does this wondrous ingredient of wondrous power wondrously manage, of itself, and without the aid of human hands, to find its way to and into the ampulla, or to withdraw from it, as often as needed?

The drollest attempt at a solution, in this line, which we remember to have met, was one put forward, with the usual air of positive assertion, in a bitter anti-Catholic magazine, published years ago in the United States, which undertook to impugn this miracle. HOT WATER, the writer maintained, was stealthily introduced into the hollow metal stem or handle below the reliquary; the heat from which might pass, by conduction, through the intervening substances, and at last reach the substance itself within the ampulla and cause it to melt.

The stem aforesaid is just three inches and one-eighth in length, and seven-eighths of an inch in external diameter. Allowing the metal of which it is formed to be one-sixteenth of an inch in thickness—less it can scarcely be—and that the hollow extends the entire length—on which point we avow our ignorance—the cavity of the stem would hold about one-fifth of a gill—rather too small a quantity for the purpose in view.

Moreover, the opening or mouth of the hollow stem is at its lower extremity. Now, inasmuch as even hot water is subject to the laws of gravity and will fall downwards, we submit that for the hot water to remain in the stem or cylinder with its lower extremity quite open, for even ten minutes, would be as truly a miracle as the liquefaction itself is claimed to be. Even allowing some invisible plug to be used to close that opening and to prevent the water from falling down, would not the first and most powerful effect of the heat of the water be manifested in the thin metallic sides of the stem itself, scorching and blistering the hands of the priest that held it?

And again, when the liquefaction is delayed—which, on this supposition, would occur because the heat in the small quantity of water first introduced is not sufficient for the purpose, and has been absorbed by the metal reliquary before producing the desired liquefaction—it would obviously become necessary to empty the stem and to take in a fresh supply of hot water. The same thing would, at least on a cold day, have to be repeated over and over again until the liquefaction finally does occur; and would have to be repeated still over again as often as the substance in the vial grows hard during the day, and a fresh liquefaction is required. Where is the vase into which they pour out the water that has lost its heat? Did any one ever see the kettle brought in with the fresh supply of water, steaming hot, as needed?

Perhaps the author of this explanation was a wag, making game of the gullible readers of the anti-Catholic magazine. If he was in earnest, we regret that he did not turn his brilliant talents to the task of discovering perpetual motion.

Lest the reader may think that we are not doing justice to the opponents of the liquefaction, we will quote the words of one who is or should be held as a high authority in their ranks. Bishop Douglas (of Salisbury, England) published A CRITERION *for distinguishing the Miracles of the New Testament from the Tricks of Pagan and Papal Priests.* Speaking of the liquefaction, he says:

"The particular natural cause is not indeed absolutely agreed upon. Some have imagined that the heat of the hands of the priests who have been tampering with the vial of blood during the celebration of Mass will be sufficient to make it melt. Others, again, have been inclined to believe that the liquefaction is affected by the heat of vast numbers of wax tapers of enormous size with which the altar is decked out, and many of which are placed so conveniently that the priest can, without any appearance of design, hold the glass so near to them as to make it hot, and consequently dis-

pose the enclosed substance to melt. I should be inclined to subscribe to this opinion, had I not met with a more probable solution.

"I am informed (for I have never tried the experiment myself) that a composition of *crocus martis* and *cochineal* will perfectly resemble congealed blood, and, by dropping the smallest quantity of *aqua fortis* amongst this composition, its dry particles will be put into a ferment, till at last an ebullition is excited and the substance becomes liquid.

"That a glass may be so contrived as to keep the *aqua fortis* from the dry substance till the critical moment when the liquefaction is to be effected may be easily conceived. And indeed the vial containing the pretended blood is so constituted. It is something like an hourglass, and the dry substance is lodged in the upper division. Now, in the lower division of the glass, a few drops of *aqua fortis* may be lodged without furnishing any suspicion, as the color will prevent its being distinguished. All the attendant circumstances of this bungling trick are perfectly well accounted for by admitting this solution. Whenever the priest would have the miracle take effect, he need only invert the glass, and then the *aqua fortis*, being uppermost, will drop down on the dry substance and excite an ebullition, which resembles the melting. And upon restoring the glass to its former position, the spectators will see the substance, the particles of which have been separated by the *aqua fortis*, drop down to the bottom of the glass, in the same manner that the sands run through an hour-glass.

"Now, upon the supposition that I have assigned the real cause, the priests can prevent the success of this miracle whenever they please; and accordingly we know that they do actually do so, when they have any prospect of advancing their own interest, by infusing a notion into the minds of the Neapolitans that heaven is angry with their nation."

Bishop Douglas with his reliquary "something like an hour-glass" deserves to stand next to him who filled the stem with boiling water. They both seem to value the dreamy supposition which they evolve out of their own inner consciousness as fully equal to undoubted and actual facts demonstrated by experience or fully established by testimony.

We leave aside the chemistry involved in his supposition, since he candidly avowed that he never tried the experiment. It is a pity he did not make a similar candid avowal when speaking of the shape of the vial containing the blood. He should, for the sake of good faith, have warned his readers that he had never seen the vial itself, nor even an engraving of it; and should have let them understand that his whole explanation was based on his assumed ability to describe accurately and minutely the shape of a vial which, he must have been aware, and should have informed them, he was entirely ignorant of.

Any one who has seen the reliquary and the ampulla within it, or has even looked at the figure of it which we have given, or at engravings of it which are easily obtained in Naples and elsewhere, will see at a glance that the shape of the ampulla is just the reverse of an hourglass. In fact, in form it much more closely approaches a sphere. Not a single point set forth in the explanation is correct. There is no upper division in which the dry substance, compounded of *crocus martis* and *cochineal*, and perfectly resembling congealed blood, is or can be lodged; there is no lower division, unoccupied save by the few drops of aqua fortis, the color of which prevents its being discovered, even by keen, curious, prying eyes. There is in the liquefaction no sandlike fall, from an upper into a lower division, of a stream of particles of the dry substance, now separated or liquefied by the aqua fortis. The bishop has not only failed to hit the bull's eye, he has entirely missed the target, every shot.

And yet, with what delicious complacency he considers, and expects his readers to admit, that he, above all others, has correctly exposed the bungling trick, and has unmasked the fraudulent dealings of the priests, who can effect or prevent the miracle as they please! It is a genuine sample of the way in which a certain class of writers think they demolish anything Catholic. And how many, after reading this passage of the *Criterion*, may have closed the book in perfect confidence that, after such an exposure, so clear and detailed, by so learned and so respectable an authority, it would be waste of time to read another word on the liquefaction of the blood of St. Januarius!

Need we go back to the two previous explanations he mentions, but which he will not adopt, until he is forced by the failure of his pet explanation? So many others have urged them that we may not pass them entirely unnoticed.

The ordinary form of the first one is this: The officiating priest, who holds in his hands the vial containing the blood, rubs it with his handkerchief, and clasps it in his palms. The animal heat of his hands, and such heat as the friction may produce, suffices to bring about the liquefaction.

Let the reader cast an eye on the very correct figure of the reliquary which we give. The priest holds it by the stem below; sometimes, in turning it, he may put one hand on the crown above. He does not, for he cannot, touch the interior vials containing the blood. They are inside the case, held in position by the soldering above and below, and are enclosed and protected by the thick metal rim, and the plates of glass in front and rear. The heat of his hands, as he holds it, and the utmost heat that can be produced by the friction—as occasionally, every five or ten minutes, he may, if he thinks it necessary, rub the plates of glass with his white handkerchief, in order to see better through them into the interior—cannot possibly affect the contents of the ampulla in any appreciable degree. As for causing them to melt or liquefy, one might as well expect the same animal heat of one's hand to light a wax candle by simply grasping and holding the candlestick in which it stands, or that lightly rubbing the candlestick with a handkerchief, every five or ten minutes, to keep it bright and dry, would produce the same physical effect on the candle placed in it as ordinary mortals obtain nowadays by igniting a lucifer match and applying it to the wick.

No one who has ever witnessed the liquefaction can listen to this attempt at explanation without a smile of pity or of contempt. Even in those cases in which the liquefactions take place while the reliquary is in the hands of the priest, it is equally insufficient and absurd. It has no application whatever to the other many cases in which the liquefaction occurs while the reliquary stands on the altar or is borne in procession. Like the other solutions we have examined, it makes no attempt to account for the reiterated hardenings and liquefactions which may occur during the day, nor for the variations of volume and for the other phases which are presented. Yet we must bear in mind that all these are striking and characteristic points, which are to be strictly accounted for, equally with the simple fact of a solid substance becoming fluid.

As for the second mode of solution mentioned by Bishop Douglas, that which attributes the liquefaction to the general heat around the altar due to the " vast number of wax tapers of enormous size " burning on the altar, and also, not to omit what others have said, to the crowd closely packed around the officiating clergyman—that attempted solution has already been disposed of. Thermometrical investigations by scientific professors, and the many times that the liquefaction takes place at the altar when there is little or no crowd, and also away from the altar and its " wax tapers of enormous size" during a procession in the streets, and while the reliquary is freely exposed to the open air of December—all alike combine to exclude this solution. As for the convenient position in which the bishop places some of those wax tapers, and the practice of the priests to make use of this position and, " without any appearance of design," to "hold the glass so near to them as to make it hot, and consequently dispose the enclosed substance to melt, " we may ask, if he did not believe this to be true, why has he repeated the statement, and expressed his inclination " to subscribe to this opinion " even as a *pis aller?* If he did believe that the priest really so manipulated the vial in order to produce the liquefaction, ought not that to be sufficient? Why postpone the truth in favor of a pet theory about *crocus martis, cochineal, aqua fortis,* and the *hour-glass?* Evidently, his mind was rather cloudy on the subject. Seriously, the priest could not hold the reliquary so near to a lighted wax taper of enormous size, long enough to make it hot, without attracting the attention of hundreds each time he did it. Not to overlook the smallest point, we may remark that, on the six occasions when we were present at the liquefaction, on all of which it invariably occurred at the main altar of the *Tesoro* chapel, the lighted tapers on the altar were few. If our memory serves us right, they were just *six,* three on each side of the crucifix over the centre of the altar, and all of them placed on tall and elevated altar candlesticks. The nearest blaze must have been, at least, seven feet away from and above the reliquary, as the chaplain held it in front of the altar. To achieve the feat which Bishop Douglas mentions, it would have been necessary to move back a portion of the crowd, near the altar, in order to get room, and then to bring in and make use of a good-sized step-ladder! The only burning light ever held in proximity to the reliquary is the single small taper, sometimes held by an assistant chaplain, and used on cloudy or hazy days, when the general light in the *Tesoro* chapel is not sufficiently strong to show through the glass plates of the reliquary and the sides of the ampulla, as distinctly as desired, the state of the blood in the interior of the ampulla. In such cases, this taper is now and then brought for half a minute or a minute within eight or ten inches of the reliquary, and is held a little higher up, and behind it, in such position that its light may shine obliquely downward through the glasses, on the surface of the blood, and show, as we saw it show, the state of the interior with perfect distinctness. It is not applied to the reliquary in any way that can appreciably heat it. When the atmosphere is perfectly clear, the general light of the chapel is amply sufficient, and this taper is not needed nor brought forward.

What we have said of the modes thus examined is true of all attempted explanations based on some supposed feat of jugglery or legerdemain during the exposition. To one who has witnessed the liquefaction at Naples, and knows what is really done, they are simply ridiculous. We repeat: if nothing else can be urged, the miracle must stand.

This has been felt, and in consequence we have another class of proposed solutions, of a seemingly higher character. Chemistry is brought into service. Some compound is skilfully prepared, we are told, and inserted by the priests into the ampulla beforehand. It is of such a character that it appears more or less hard and solid at the beginning of the exposition, and, during the exposition, is made to melt or to appear to melt. Chemists, we are assured, can easily prepare such substances, and can thus reproduce the liquefactions at will. These experiments, it is claimed, settle the question. What the chemists do and acknowledge, the priests do, and pass off as a miracle.

Let us analyze these experiments, and see whether in reality they repeat and renew the liquefaction with its characteristic and essential phenomena, or in what respects and how far they fail to do so.

The first of these of which we have any account dates from Berlin, in 1734. On the 26th of January in that year—so we are told in a letter dated a few days after, and published in Paris — Gaspar Neumann, councillor of his majesty's court, doctor in medicine, and professor of chemistry, entertained a party consisting of fourteen learned friends, assembled to dine at his festive board, with an imitation of the liquefaction of the blood of St. Januarius. The letter was written by one of the party to his friends at home. We carefully reproduce the facts which the letter states, omitting the badinage and sneering remarks with which it accompanies them — remarks quite characteristic of the school of Voltaire whenever religion or anything connected with it was in question. In default of the original French, we quote from a translation published in England.

The professor, we are told, placed before his friends " a human skull." He also produced from his laboratory " three vials of crystal or very clear and transparent glass, in each of which was contained a matter in a very small bulk, dry, black, and so hard as to produce a noise on the sides of the vial when shaken." The first vial being brought near to the head, the matter in it " became of a deep-red color, liquefied, bubbled, increased its bulk, and filled the vial." The second vial was also brought near to the head, and the portion of matter in it " bubbled but little." But when the third vial was similarly brought near the head, the whole of its contents " remained dry, hard, and black."

The writer evidently wished to convey the impression—perhaps he himself believed — that these vials, which the professor had carefully prepared in his laboratory and showed to his friends after dinner, correctly exhibited the liquefaction in all its chief phases. If the liquid in the first vial had also several times changed its color ; if it had filled the vial, not by adding bubbles to bubbles, but by an actual increase of the volume of the liquid within, independently of that frothing or bubbling ; if it had then similarly decreased in bulk ; if the liquid had solidified without any diminution of temperature, and become fluid again without increase of it, he would have presented a far stronger case than he has done.

But those points are absent. Perhaps the writer did not know that they were necessary. The letter itself is written in a jocular and mocking tone, and evidently in a spirit that relished sharp epigrammatic points, calculated to excite a laugh, far more than the humdrum reality of sober truth.

We find another account of this same experiment in a French work before us : *La Liquefaction du Sang de S. Janvier*, by Postel. This account is more calm and sober in style, and is based upon the *Bibliothèque Germanique*, a work to which we have not access. It varies considerably from the sportive account given in the letter. According to Postel, the contents of the first vial *liquefied entirely ;* the contents of the second vial *liquefied only partially ;* in the third vial there was *no change whatever.* The statement is distinctly made that neither in the first vial nor in the second was there any sign of ebullition. The variation is important.

As between the two accounts, we could scarcely hesitate a moment which to hold most worthy of credit on any point on which they differed. In neither account do we find any indication of the nature of the chemical compounds which Dr. Neumann had prepared in his laboratory and placed in the vials. But as the experiment was made known and repeated, especially in France, we may take it for granted that the material used in those repetitions is the same that he devised.

This material is a mixture of suet, or other similar fatty matter, and ether, the compound being brought to any desired tint—in this case, a deep or dark red—by a further admixture of any suitable pigment. The mixture or compound so prepared is solid at ordinary temperatures; but at about 92° F. it will melt. If a quantity of such a mixture be inserted in a small glass vial, and the vial be clasped in the palm of one's hand, it will soon receive from the hand sufficient heat to bring about a total or a partial liquefaction, according to the greater or smaller proportion of the ether used in originally compounding it.

Neither would it be beyond the art of chemistry, in preparing this mixture, to introduce other ingredients, the particles of which would be brought into contact with each other when the liquefaction has been effected and the chemical combinations of which would then give rise to a greater or less amount of frothing or bubbles.

All this, however, is very far from being a reproduction of the liquefaction which is seen at Naples. The differences, or rather the failures to imitate and reproduce it, are essential and evident. We point out the chief ones :

I. This liquefaction of the laboratory *always and entirely* depends on the application of the proper degree of heat. So long as its temperature is below the melting point, the substance in the vial remains hard and unliquefied. When the temperature, from whatsoever cause, is raised above that degree, liquefaction ensues. If the temperature again sinks below it, the substance, if not meanwhile decomposed, returns to its previous solid condition. The operators themselves inform us frankly how the required degree of heat is usually communicated to it; by holding the vial, if small enough, in the palm of one hand, or tightly pressing it, if somewhat larger, between the palms of both hands. If the general heat of the room be raised high enough to reach the melting point of the substance in the vial, this circumstance alone would suffice to bring the compound to a fluid condition.

On the other hand, being from Naples and not from Brobdignag, the chaplain or canon has a hand only of the ordinary size, and is alto-gether unable to clasp in the palm of one hand, or even with both palms, an object so large as the reliquary. He is forced to hold it by the stem ; in which position, the heat of his hand can have no appreciable effect on the contents of the vial within the reliquary.

Moreover, the liquefaction often takes place when the reliquary is not held in his hands at all.

II. We repeat it again. The real liquefaction does not depend on heat It takes place at various temperatures. There is no fixed melting point for the substance in the ampulla. It will often solidify at a higher temperature than that at which it stood liquid; and will liquefy at a temperature notably below that at which it became or stood solid. This is an essential difference, going to the root of the question.

III. The attempted imitation may, at the utmost, present a bubbling or frothing, produced in the way we have indicated. This may even go to such an extent as to fill the vial with froth or bubbles. But it can never cause the bulk or body of the liquid itself, free from those bubbles, and independently of them, to swell and increase in actual visible amount so as to completely fill the vial. The amount of the liquid obtained, when at rest and in its tranquil state, and at the same temperature, will always be the same. Precisely the reverse happens in the liquefaction of the blood of St. Januarius. The liquid blood may bubble and froth without increasing its bulk, or it may increase its volume with or without this frothing, or it may decrease its volume, again, with or without the frothing. And these changes of the bulk of the actual liquid in the ampulla do not depend on the temperature. Neither are they points on which a mistake is possible; for they reach, as we have stated, to the extent of twenty per cent.

On those two cardinal points, the imitation entirely fails. We need scarcely note the facts that the preparation, when solid, does not resemble coagulated or hardened blood, and, when liquid, could never be mistaken for liquid blood, whether arterial or venous, nor does it present the changes of color so often seen in the real liquefaction.

IV. Ether is an essential ingredient of this artificial compound. Suet, or whatever other fatty substance is used instead, will dissolve in ether; while it will not dissolve in water or in alcohol. Now, ether is comparatively a modern discovery. Whether Paracelsus hit upon the discovery of it or not is a point mooted among those who have studied his life and achievements in chemistry. But, if he did, the knowledge of it was lost with him, and it remained unknown to the world until Künkel discovered or rediscovered it in 1681—early enough for Neumann, but entirely too late to be of any service in getting up a compound for the liquefaction at Naples, which, for the matter of that, runs back far beyond the days of Paracelsus himself.

This explanation, therefore, that the liquefaction of the blood of St. Januarius is in reality the liquefaction of a compound of ether and suet or other fatty substance, must be set aside, because entirely insufficient to meet the case, and because it involves a glaring anachronism.

It fails, too, in another point. The ether will, in course of time, gradually escape though the pores of the glass. When it is gone, the liquefactions are at an end. The fatty matters, too, will decompose in time. In fact, the whole preparation would have to be frequently renewed. On the other hand, as we shall see further on, there is ample evidence that the ampulla remains unopened, and that the substance within it remains untouched and identically the same, from year to year, and from century to century.

These reasons were too patent to allow Dr. Neumann's attempted imitation to hold its own in the estimation of those who seriously examined the question. It was thrown aside for others. We find an account of one of them, written by La Condamine, and presented to no less a body than the Academy of Sciences in Paris, in 1757. His article may be found among the various articles published in the *Memoirs* for 1763.

La Condamine explains, with no little glee, and some detail, an experiment which he had lately witnessed in company with others, and which he was allowed afterward to repeat and study out in private and at his leisure, and with the assistance and explanations of the inventor himself. He does not give the inventor's name, but we know, from other sources, that it was San Severo.

There was a circular case of bronze or silver gilt. In front and rear, there were circular plates of glass. The whole stood on a richly ornamented foot, and was surmounted by a winged mercury. Within the case, between the plates of glass, was seen a vial. So far, the workman had prepared a vague imitation of the actual reliquary.

" The vial appeared half full of a stiff grayish paste, which, judging by its surface, seemed to be powdery or granulated. By inclining the case, alternately, from side to side, and shaking it for half a minute, more or less, the paste became liquid and flowing, sometimes only partially so; at other times, it grew hard again, and by shaking it anew it became liquid again. . . . I remarked beneath the vial two small cones, I do not know of what material, meeting by their points.

I was told (by the inventor) that there was a little passage through these points. He said, also, that the cones were hollow, and that, as the lower one was movable, it sometimes happened that its orifice exactly met the orifice of the upper cone, and sometimes did not; this was altogether a matter of chance. . . . As for the powder which I saw in the vial, I was told that it was an amalgam of mercury, lead, tin, and bismuth; that the bismuth, which amalgamated only imperfectly, hindered the mixture from becoming a pasty lump, and gave it rather the character of a powder too coarse to pass through the little opening which communicated with the cones. Finally, there was hidden, within the case, a circular tube communicating with the lower movable cone, and containing liquid mercury. In shaking the whole irregularly, whenever the openings of the two cones came together, more or less of this mercury made its way into the vial and liquefied the amalgam. It happened sometimes, in these various movements, that the mercury which had entered got out again, and then the amalgam returned to its previous condition and was fluid no longer."

This is the account which La Condamine has given, after a long and careful private examination, aided by the explanations of the inventor, and which, he tells us, he wrote down the same day. The inventor promised to give him in writing a fuller account, with minute drawings of all the parts; but up to the date of publication (five years later) he had, for some unknown reason, failed to keep the promise.

La Condamine acknowledges that he had never seen the real reliquary, and had never witnessed the true liquefaction at Naples. He thought this substitute just as good.

Had he witnessed the reality, and had he examined it with one-half the care he bestowed on the substitute, he never would have written his report.

I. He would have instantly seen the difference between a true lique-faction—where a substance previously hard is unmistakably seen to become gradually soft and then perfectly liquid, as is often the case at Naples—and this seeming liquefaction of the experiment, which consists only in making the loosened grains or particles of the amalgam swim in and on the fluid mercury which has been introduced, they themselves remaining hard and not at all liquefied, but ready to be heaped together again in a hard mass of grains or powder, whenever the liquid mercury is withdrawn. The difference between the two processes is as clear as light, and as great as the difference between the melting of icebergs and a movement of a fleet of ships on the ocean. A child could not mistake it. Fortunately, the icebergs melt and disappear as they are changed into water: with equal good fortune, the ships do not melt, but float on, until they reach their port.

II. He would see that this grayish amalgam, in its dry, powdery state, is totally unlike the hard, dark mass of blood in the ampulla, and, in its pretended liquid state, it is equally unlike the liquid blood. In fact, as the mercury enters below and permeates the mass, its silvery gleam may somewhat enliven the dull-grayish hue of the amalgam, but it can present nothing akin to the *rubicund*, the *bright vermilion*, or the *dark hue* of the liquid blood. Nor is there anything like the film which the liquid blood sometimes leaves on the sides of the glass, nor like the frothing, or the ebullition. On all these points, the experiment failed.

III. After sufficient mercury has been introduced to occupy the interstices in the granular mass, any additional supply will lift the particles, separate them, and allow that motion which the inventor passed off for fluidity; and this seeming fluidity becomes greater as the quantity of fluid mercury so introduced for the grains to float in is increased in amount. But the mercury occupies space, and so increase of bulk and increased fluidity must go together. A hardening requires, on the contrary, a withdrawal of the mercury, and is consequently always connected with a decrease of bulk. This is directly contrary to one of the most striking features of the real liquefaction, on which we have already commented at length.

IV. It fails to account for the hardenings and the liquefactions which occur when the reliquary is not in the hands of a chaplain or canon to incline it never so coaxingly, but stands and has been standing for hours, untouched and immovable, on its pedestal on the altar. In this point the imitation again signally fails.

V. What we said of ether, we may almost repeat here concerning the bismuth. This is the important ingredient of the amalgam, the intractableness of which keeps the material in a state of powder or grains. When that is overcome, the whole mass coheres and becomes a hard lump; and the liquefactions, such as they were, are over. Now, bismuth was discoved by Agricola in 1529, centuries after the date when the liquefactions are known to have regularly occurred.

VI. The prying eyes of thousands have never discovered in the reliquary any trace of a circular tube containing mercury, nor of the all-important little hollow cones, meeting by their points. More than once, as we shall see, the reliquary has been in the hands of goldsmiths and skilled workmen. They found nothing of this nor of any other contrivance.

These two of Neumann and San Severo are the chief attempts made to imitate the liquefaction of the blood of St. Januarius, and they have signally failed. We need not examine, one by one, the various substances which have been proposed as the chemical substance craftily used on this occasion; from the "deep-red sublimate of gold," which, one tells us, "being easily fusible by the heat of one's hand, is exhibited by the Neapolitan priests for St. Januarius's blood," down to the theory that "the dark-red mass which melts in the ampulla is only a preparation of ICE; for everybody knows that in Naples they are more skilful in preparing ices than even in Archangel." By the way, we suspect that Aulic Councillor Rehfues, a German Protestant traveller, to whom we owe this last explanation, was only making fun of his brother Aulic Councillor Neumann, and of the other theorists, who were proposing, each one, his own guess as to the substance.

Anyway, the fact that the real liquefaction is not caused by the application of heat rules out all these suppositions. The fuller and more accurate our knowledge of chemistry, the more clearly do we realize the truth that all experimental liquefactions are governed by the laws of nature. The more conversant we are with the *facts* of the real liquefaction, the more clearly do we see that here those laws are set aside. We cannot shut our eyes to the opposition.

Sir Humphry Davy, who witnessed the liquefaction when he visited Naples, and who carefully examined it, made no secret afterwards among his friends of the deep impression it produced on his mind, and of his decided judgment that chemistry, so far as he knew it, could not account for the liquefaction. This may have been one of the causes of that inclination toward the Catholic Church which, from the period of that visit, was manifested by that eminent scholar, and which led him to think seriously, at least, of entering her fold, even if he did not—as some thought he did—carry his purpose into effect before death.

And yet we are asked to believe that, " away back in the dark ages," those " ignorant monks and priests in Naples " possessed a knowledge of chemistry which enabled them to do this! And, more wonderful still, that they have secretly handed down that knowledge and power, within their own body, and that they continue to this day to effect the liquefaction in some strange way entirely unknown to the scientific world !

We pass on to other views of the question.

This charge of fraud implies that the ampulla is tampered with from time to time ; and that those who have charge of it—clergy and laity alike—and especially those who hold it at the time of the liquefaction, are all playing a trick.

Is the ampulla or vial really tampered with ? Is it regularly opened for the insertion of some duly prepared material ?

The ampulla stands within a case or reliquary, as our figure shows it. The case or reliquary, of silver and of glass, is kept in an *Armoire,* or closet, wrought in the solid stone wall of the *Tesoro* chapel, as strong and secure as a bank-vault. This *Armoire* is closed by metal doors, each secured by two strong locks, with different keys, one set of which is always in the possession of the municipal authorities of the city, the other in that of the archbishop and clergy. They have been so kept for just two hundred and twenty-four years ; for we need not take account just now of the previous centuries, when the relics were in the exclusive custody of the archbishop and clergy, and were kept in the old *Tesoro,* or strong room, still to be seen in the second story of the cathedral tower. During all these two hundred and twenty-four years, the locks have not been tampered with. The clergy have not charged any one with doing it. The municipal authorities have never suspected it.

Moreover, the reliquary, when brought out, remains exposed to public scrutiny for ten or twelve hours at a time, on eighteen days of each year ; and there is no man, woman, or child in Naples, and no stranger in the city, who may not, if so minded, scrutinize it a score of times a day, at less than twelve inches' distance. Any opening or closing of the case, any taking out or putting in of the vial, would leave some trace of the fact, either in the silver rim, or in the position of the vials within, or at least in the soldering at bottom and at top, which would have to be disturbed, if not broken, each time, and then restored. Among the special industries of Naples are working in jewelry and coral, retouching and repairing paintings, and—we are sorry to say it—fabricating *Old Masters.* The Neapolitans have eyes for signs and traces like these in question as quick, sharp, and unerring as an Indian on a trail. No change or trace of any tampering has ever been seen by them. The vials are in identically the same inclined position from year to year—the same as represented in engravings a century or two centuries old. The soldering, in which the bottoms and tops are immersed, is hard, old, black, through age, and evidently untouched. The outer case shows no sign of any opening by which a side can be unscrewed or lifted out, so as to allow the vials themselves to be touched. Probably, when originally made, five hundred and fifty or seven hundred years ago, this could have been done. But the screw or the joint has long since rusted, and the whole thing is now one mass of dingy and rusted silver, holding two glass plates.

In the year 1649, Cardinal Ascanio Filomarini was Archbishop of Naples, a man of great culture and taste and of ample private fortune, and much given to the adornment of the churches of his diocese.

The new *Tesoro* had just been completed, and was shining in all the brilliant splendor of newness. The cardinal thought that the reliquary to contain the vials of the blood, for which the *Tesoro* had been built, ought to correspond, as the bust did, with the grandeur of the chapel itself. This the dingy old silver reliquary, in which they had been kept for so many centuries, did not do. He determined to replace it by another of gold, of excellent workmanship, and adorned with rich jewels. He had one made "regardless of expense," and, when all was ready, on September 1, 1649, he came into the *Tesoro* with some of his clergy and the delegates from the city, and with public notaries, that proper legal record might be made of everything, and with chosen goldsmiths. Are not the names of them all duly recorded? The *Armoire* was opened, the reliquary was taken to the adjoining sacristy; and there, for several hours, in presence of his eminence and his clergy, and the honorable delegates, "and of us, the undersigned notaries," the goldsmiths tried and essayed to open the reliquary. They failed and gave it up. They could break the reliquary, if so directed; but they could not open it. Accordingly, the reliquary was locked up again as it had been taken out. The cardinal was a persevering man. He got other goldsmiths, and came a

second time, on the 8th of September, with clergy, delegates, and notaries. For two hours again these goldsmiths tried to open the reliquary, and failed, as the first had done. They could break it, if required; but how could they open a case where all their trying could find neither joint nor screw? Again the reliquary was replaced in the *Armoire*. The cardinal's heart was set on using his new grand reliquary on the festival near at hand, the 19th of September. He thought over the matter, again summoned the delegates and the notaries, and on the 16th came, a third time, with his clergy and yet other goldsmiths. A third prolonged trial was made with the same ill-success. The reliquary might be broken, if they wished; it could not be opened. To break it was not to be thought of; that might endanger the precious vials within. So, the old silver reliquary was put up again, that evening, and his eminence was forced to use it on the festival of the 19th for the exposition that year. It has been used ever since. And now, two hundred and twenty-two years later, it was again brought out on the 19th of September in this present year, 1871. The cardinal, it is to be presumed, devoted his rich reliquary to some other pious purpose.

But if his eminence had lived to the age of the olden patriarchs, and had retained it in his possession, he might have at last found a more favorable opportunity for again trying to change that reliquary. On the afternoon of Tuesday, May 5, 1762, one of the glass plates, by dint, of course, of being rubbed for so many hundred years by white handkerchiefs, became somewhat loose in its groove or socket, and threatened to fall inward, endangering the precious vials. Accordingly, early next morning, an hour and a half before the time for the regular exposition (for it was in the May octave), the archbishop of that day, Cardinal Sersale, came with clergy, city delegates, notaries-public, and goldsmiths. The reliquary was taken out of the *Armoire*, and the glass was fixed again firmly in its place, and the reliquary was returned to its *Armoire,* before the hour for the public exposition. It does not appear, from the very succinct account we have of the occurrence, whether or not, during the work, the vials or ampullæ were taken out of the reliquary, within which they are held in their places by the old soldering. Nothing is said of this having been done, nor of the soldering being touched and then repaired when they were put back in their places. On the whole, considering the nature of the repair to be done, and that it was done in a few moments at the door of the *Armoire,* back of the altar, we are inclined to think that they did not find it necessary to move them, and that they were accordingly left untouched in their places.

These are the only occasions on which the diaries say anything bearing on the feasibility of opening this reliquary, or of its being repaired. In the archives of the cathedral, another incident is mentioned, of an ancient date. In the year 1507, nearly a century and a half before the building of the new *Tesoro,* the relics were kept in the old *Tesoro* or strong room of the cathedral, a strong vaulted chamber of stone, in the second story of the tower, which rises at the northeast corner of the church. That *Tesoro* was then approached by a winding stairway. A very aged canon was bringing down the reliquary from the *Tesoro* to the church for an exposition. At the very first step, he tripped and fell; and the reliquary rolled down, from

step to step, to the very bottom. All present feared it was broken, and gave thanks when it was taken up and found to be perfectly uninjured. Yet the alarm had been great; and Maria Toleta, " the pious wife of the viceroy," who was present at the time and shared in the alarm, had the winding stairway taken down at her own expense, and replaced by another one, straight, broad, and easy, which is in use to this day.

We may take these facts as fair evidence that the reliquary is strong, and not very easily opened, and that they who know all about it do not believe that it is or can be regularly opened.

The same conclusion is also forced on us by considerations of an entirely different character. We have already drawn attention to the fact that, whatever the level at which the blood stands when the reliquary is locked up at night, at the close of one exposition—whether *at its ordinary level,* or *somewhat increased,* or *very much increased,* or *full*—it is invariably found at the same level when taken out the next time for the ensuing exposition, whether that time be next morning or after the lapse of months. The level is one of the points specially noticed and recorded. A variation would necessarily be detected. Yet, if on each one or on very many of the four thousand occasions we have spoken of, the old contents had been privately taken out between the expositions, and a fresh supply put in, would there not have been, not unfrequently, some appreciable inequality of level?

Again, sometimes the blood was *hard* when put up. How could a hard substance be extracted from a narrow-necked vial of glass without breaking it? According to our tables, on three different occasions the blood, after its usual liquefactions and changes in September, *filled* the ampulla, and was so locked up at the end of the novena. It was found *full* and *hard* in December following, and, not liquefying at all, was again locked up in the same condition. It was found in precisely the same state when the reliquary was again taken out in the May following. Here, on three occasions, the contents of the vial, solid and completely filling it, must have remained unextracted from September to May, seven months. Yet in the May octaves that followed, the liquefactions went on as usual. No freshly inserted compound was necessary for the liquefaction. The same reasoning applies · in a measure to the numerous cases in which such a fulness went over, four months and a half, from May to September, or nearly three months, from September to December.

Again, in quite a number of instances, as the same tables show, the condition of the blood, when locked up, is noted as *liquid with a floating hard lump*, as was the case on the 16th of December, 1870. When it was taken out, the next day, or after several months, though often found entirely hardened, yet not unfrequently—as on the 6th of May, 1871—it was found in precisely the same state in which it had been put up: *liquid with a floating hard lump*. In all these cases, the condition of the contents of the ampulla is a new and insuperable objection to the supposition that a newly prepared amount of matter had been inserted for the subsequent liquefactions. Did other circumstances allow it, we might conceive a liquid to be poured out of the ampulla, and a fresh liquid to be poured in. But how is the solid hard lump, that would not liquefy, to be got out? And if got out, how is another hard lump to be put in to replace it? Are the constituents of

this new hard lump poured into the ampulla separately, as liquids or powders that can pass through the neck? Then their character must be such that, instead of uniting with the liquid already there, or the constituents of the liquid portion, they will, on the contrary, combine apart to form the hard mass. But if so antagonistic to the liquid portion, how is it that, when the lump does liquefy during the ensuing exposition, these constituents at once intimately unite with the liquid, the whole forming a homogeneous mass, which without the least indication of any antagonism between its component parts will henceforth solidify and liquefy as a single mass?

The more carefully the facts of the case are studied, the more imperatively do they exclude every hypothesis save the simple one which so many other facts corroborate, that no attempt has been made to change the contents of the ampulla. Everything about the ampulla excludes the idea that it is regularly tampered with privately between the expositions.

There is still another light in which we must view this charge of fraud. Ever since the opening of the new *Tesoro*, in 1646, there have been attached to that chapel twelve chaplains and a *custos*, with inferior attendants as needed. In the cathedral itself, at least from 1496, there have been twenty canons and beneficiaries, besides minor attendants. When the liquefaction takes place in the *Tesoro*, the reliquary is in the hands of the chaplains, who act in turn, or relieve each other as convenient. When it occurs in the procession or in the cathedral, or in some other church, the reliquary is in the charge of the canons, who similarly relieve each other. Hence, canons and chaplains, all alike, must be cognizant of the fraud, if any there be, and must participate in it. Add to these the archbishops and their vicars-general in Naples since 1496. Add also those clergymen who, having been canons or chaplains, have passed to other dignities, or have retired from their office, but must of course still retain the knowledge of this fraud, if they once possessed it. We may say that there have been on an average, at all times, forty ecclesiastics, if not more, who had cognizance of the fraud, if there were any. The dignity of canon of the cathedral or chaplain of the *Tesoro* is ordinarily reached only after years of meritorious service in the lower grades of the ministry. Hence the canons and chaplains are usually men of mature and advanced age. We can scarcely give them more than fifteen years of average life. We have thus about a thousand clergymen since A.D. 1500, all charged with being cognizant of and participators in the fraud.

Now, what was the character of those men? Those among whom they lived, and who knew them, respected them as a body of men devoted to the service of God, pure and exemplary ecclesiastics, proved by years spent in the zealous works of the ministry. Some were men of honorable and noble families; others were men distinguished in the walks of literature and science; some had sacrificed all the world promised them, in order to spend their lives in the sanctuary. Some were revered in life, and remembered after death, as pre-eminently true servants of God, men of prayer, of strong faith, and of singularly pure and saintly lives. Of course, individuals here or there may indeed have been wicked or hypocritical. But this testimony of the people to their character must have been true of the great body.

Now, could such men have all united in this fraud? On their own principles and convictions, and according to the doctrines they taught and should themselves practise, there could scarcely be a more heinous sin against God and his holy religion, than to palm off a trick of crafty men as a miracle of God's working. Could they bring themselves to it?

Is it possible that no one of them ever repented, even in the presence of death, and sought to save his soul, and to make reparation, by disclosing the fraud and arresting the evil? Could all have chosen to die impenitent, with the certainty of everlasting damnation before them, rather than reveal the blasphemous and, to them, henceforth useless trick? The thing is impossible.

Again, men, even though good and pious, may be garrulous. All men have their unguarded moments. How came it that the secret never leaked out from any one of them during all these years?

Again, among so many there must have been men wicked, avaricious, passionate, revengeful. How comes it that no one sought to make money by revealing the secret; that no one declared it through anger; that no one did so in retaliation when he was punished by his ecclesiastical superiors?

Nay, more, we fear that instances might be found in which, toward the close of the last century, some of them were carried away by the irreligious mania then prevailing, and became the companions of infidels, if not themselves infidels. And unless our memory is at fault, one or two yielded to the blandishments and the privileges of Protestantism. How comes it that, through such, the world has not learned how this antiquated trick is actually done? Obviously, they had no disclosure to make. This is the only possible answer.

There is still more to be said on this point. The civil authorities of Naples are, and have been for two hundred and twenty-four years, joint custodians with the archbishop and clergy of the *Tesoro* chapel and of the relics of St. Januarius. They keep one set of the keys of the *Armoire*, or closet, which can never be opened save in the presence of one of their members, whom they send as a delegate, and whose sworn duty it is never to lose sight of the reliquary until it is placed in its closet, and he assists in duly locking it up. During these two hundred and twenty-four years, Naples has again and again changed masters. Austrians, Lombards, Spaniards, and French—Bourbon, Imperial, and Republican—have held, as the Piedmontese now hold, the city, which in fact has oftener been ruled by strangers than by Neapolitans. These rulers have been men of every character, from the best to the worst; often rough, ruthless soldiers, who brooked no opposition, and were ever ready with the sword; often keen, crafty civilians, ready to cajole, to bribe, and to deceive, and thoroughly practised to detect plots and ferret out hidden things; sometimes professed infidels and avowed enemies of all religion; oftener political enemies of the Neapolitan clergy, whose hearts, of course, were with their own oppressed people. How comes it that none of these rulers at any time have ever discovered and made known the fraud?

Can we suppose that those rulers, ill-disposed as they often were toward the clergy, could or would sacrifice their own interests, their policy, their jealousies, and their personal feeling, in order to co-operate in a fraud, the success of which would certainly be less agreeable, perhaps far less profitable, to them, than its failure and exposure?

Would not the French infidels, in 1799, have gladly put this stigma on the odious cause of Christianity?

And, in these present years, would not Ratazzi, Garibaldi, and their party gladly do it if they could? What a triumph it would be for them if they could strike this blow at "clericalism"—a blow far more effective than fining, imprisoning, or exiling bishops and priests and religious! They would glory in doing it if it were possible. What holds them back? There are no limits to their hatred or to their powers of calumny. They are ever denouncing the ignorance and the blind superstition of priests and people. But the very gist and copiousness of their invectives prove that they themselves know and feel that the priests and people are alike sincere. It is the depth and earnestness of that sincerity which excites their rage.

Brought face to face, in Naples, with this manifestation of the supernatural, the civil government, whatever the political circumstances and whatever the private character of individual members of it, have always seemed struck with awe, and have never failed in respect. Nay, more, they have ever claimed and exercised their privilege of sending their delegate to intervene in the exposition.

And so, after all, on the 19th of this last September, as in times past, they did send a delegate, with his scarlet embroidered bag, and the two antique keys chained together; and the doors of the *Armoire* were opened; and the relics were reverently taken out and carried to the altar; and the blood was seen to be *hard*; and the clergy and the crowd prayed and waited for the miracle; "and, after eight minutes of prayer, the hard mass became entirely liquid."

There is an anecdote current in the world on this subject which we have heard cited as peremptory against much of what we have just said. The anecdote, in passing from mouth to mouth, has become so vague and so full of variations that we would scarcely know how to present it, had we not found a precise and *quasi* authoritative form of it in the columns of the *Coryphæus* of French infidelity, the *Siècle* of Paris of the date of October 11, 1856:

"The history of Championnet did some damage to the miracle of St. Januarius in the minds of a great many. In 1799, the French army was in Naples, where it had been well received at first. . . . . On the 6th of May, the crowd filled the chapel of the cathedral. . . . For more than half an hour the priest had been turning backward and foward, on his hands, the round silver lantern with two faces of glass within which is preserved the precious blood in a small vial. The little reddish mass would not quit its state of solidity. . . . The exasperated populace commenced to attribute the stubbornness of San Gennaro to the presence of the French. There was danger of a tumult, when an aid hastened to notify General Championnet of the suspicious conduct of the saint. In a few moments the aid returned, approached the priest politely, and said a few words in his ear. What he did say is not precisely known, but he had scarcely said it when the blood at once liquefied, to the great joy of the people, who at last had their miracle."

Alexandre Dumas, in one of his novels, narrates the same story much more dramatically. According to him, "General Championnet saw that it was important for his safety and the safety of the army that the miracle should not fail that year; and he made up his mind that, one way or another, it should positively occur." The first Sunday of May was near at hand. On the vigil (May 4, 1799), the procession marched, but between files of French grenadiers. That night the city was patrolled by French and Italian soldiers jointly. All day Sunday the miracle was patiently waited for; but in vain. Six in the afternoon came—Championnet, with his staff, was in his elevated *loggia* or gallery. The people began at length to lose patience and to vociferate angrily. At 7 P.M. they were brandishing knives and threatening the general, who pretended not to understand or heed them. At 8 P.M. the streets around were filled with other crowds equally threatening. "The grenadiers waited on a signal from the general to charge bayonets. The general continued unmoved." At half-past eight, as the tumult was still increasing, "the general bent over and whispered something to an aid-de-camp." The aid left the stand, and passed up to the altar and knelt in the front rank, and waited. In five minutes the canon, bearing the reliquary, came round to him in his turn. He kissed the reliquary as others did; but, while doing so, grasped the priest's hand in his.

"'Father, a word with you.'
"'What is it?' asked the priest. ·
"'I must say to you, on the part of the general commanding, that if in ten minutes the miracle is not accomplished, in fifteen minutes your reverence shall be shot.'
"The canon let the reliquary fall from his hands. Fortunately, the young officer caught it before it reached the ground, and gave it back with every mark of profound respect. Then he arose and returned to his place near the general.
"'Well?' said the general.
"'All right, general,' said the young officer. 'In ten minutes the miracle will take place.'
"The aid-de-camp spoke the truth; nevertheless he made a mistake of five minutes; for at the end of five minutes only, the canon raised the reliquary aloft, exclaiming, *Il miracolo è fatto.* The blood was completely liquefied."

We suppose we may take these as the best versions of the same story.

The other French and late English versions we have met of it, however they may vary in minor details, all agree as to the person—General Championnet, and as to the year, 1799. So far as we can judge, the *Siècle* and the other writers got their facts from the novelist. It is their way. When they attack religion, all manner of weapons are acceptable. Where the novelist got it we need scarcely inquire. Certainly, on a pinch, he was capable of inventing it out of the whole cloth. But we can only credit him with twisting and reversing an older story. In a work entitled *Naples and Campagna Felice*, printed in London in 1815, there is an earlier account of "the very recent experiment of General Championnet."

"When this *Champion* of liberty entered Naples with his unhosed *enfans de la patrie*, his curiosity, or rather his infidelity, prompted him to direct the priests forthwith to perform the ceremony before him and his companions, the philosophic worshippers of the Goddess of Reason. . . . 'The miracle must be exhibited this instant, or I'll smash your vials and all your nonsense into a thousand pieces.' . . Every devout effort of the priests proved vain ; even the general's active assistance and repeated trials to give fluidity to the indurated blood, by means of natural and artificial heat, were equally unsuccessful."

This want of success, according to the teller of the story, was due to the fact that the relatives of St. Januarius were not present. The general sent soldiers to arrest them, and had them brought into the church.

"A second experiment was now instituted in due form : which, to the utter amazement of the French part of the congregation, and to the inward delight of all the pious Neapolitans, succeeded almost instantaneously."

Were it not for the identity of names and place, we could scarcely recognize this earlier English version, with its characteristic contempt of French philosophers and *enfans de la patrie*, and its result of the experiment so satisfactory to the Neapolitans, as in reality the original form of the story, which Dumas, and after him many others, have dressed up and presented to the world with such different details, and with a result exactly opposite.

But a regard for truth obliges us to reject this earlier form, no less than those which followed, as, all of them, pure fictions. The evidence is clear and to the point.

I. On May 4, 1799, General Championnet was not in Naples. He had entered that city with his army on the 28th of January preceding, and had established "The Parthenopean Republic"; but he had been relieved of his command before May ; possibly on account of ill health, for he died at Antibes a few months later. His successor in the command at Naples was General, afterwards Marshal Macdonald.

II. The diary of the *Tesoro* chapel, and the archiepiscopal diary, in their accounts of the exposition on Saturday, May 4, 1799, both mention the presence of General Macdonald with his officers.

III. According to the same authorities, the liquefaction, so far from being long delayed, that day took place quite soon—after a lapse of only ten minutes.

IV. They indicate the very respectful demeanor of the French general, and his expressions of reverence; expressions which, by the way, he confirmed afterwards by presenting to the *Tesoro* chapel a beautiful silk mitre, rich in gold work and jewels, which is still shown in the sacristy.

V. Finally, to clinch the whole matter, we quote the following ex tract from a contemporary letter, published at the time in the official organ at Paris—the *Moniteur*, No. 259, of date 19 Prairial, Year VII. (June 10, 1799).

"Naples, 21 Floréal (May 13).—The festival of St. Januarius has just been celebrated with the customary solemnity. General Macdonald (successor to Championnet), Commissary Abrial, and all the staff, witnessed the renowned miracle. As it took place somewhat sooner than usual, the people think better of us Frenchmen, and do not look on us any more as atheists."

The writer little thought what a dramatic story a novelist's imagination would conjure up, and some credulous people would believe, instead of the simple matter-of-fact statement he gave *en passant* of the solemnity he had just witnessed. A more complete refutation of the whole story could not be desired than that afforded by the words and tone of this letter.

We have been diffuse on the charge of fraud. But when we consider the persistence with which it is made, and the variety of forms in which it is presented; and that, after all, for most minds, the alternative is between a suspicion of fraud, on one side, and the recognition of the miraculous character of the liquefaction, on the other—it was proper to treat this charge at length and in all its aspects.

We have seen that the publicity of everything about the exposition peremptorily forbids every form of leger demain during the ceremony. Equally inadmissible is the supposition of some chemical compound prepared beforehand. For no chemical compound which man can prepare will liquefy, as this does, independently of heat, and under such diverse circumstances, or will present the many varying phases which are here seen. The most artistic attempts have utterly failed, and must ever fail. For they are all subject to the laws of nature; while, in this liquefaction, the laws of nature are clearly set aside.

Again, all testimony goes to show that the ampulla is not opened from time to time to receive any chemical preparation.

Moreover, if there were any fraud, it would have been known to nearly a thousand clergymen, and no one can say to how many laymen. Yet pious men were never heard to denounce it; repentant men never disclosed it; high-minded and honorable men never repudiated it in scorn, vile and mercenary men were never moved by anger, revenge, desire of pecuniary gain, or other potent motives, to betray it. Even political enmities and fierce party strife, so prone to indulge in charges of fraud, have failed in Naples to stigmatize this as a fraud. Evidently, there was no fraud known or suspected there. In fine, were there a fraud, this universal silence would be a greater miracle than the liquefaction itself.

It has been asked, sometimes jeeringly, perhaps sometimes seriously, if the Neapolitans are in such perfect faith and so sure of the character of the substance which liquefies in the ampulla, why are they unwilling to submit that substance to the test of chemical analysis? Is not their omission, nay, their unwillingness to do this, a confession on their part of the weakness of their cause?

To one who knows them, or who even reflects for a moment on the subject, the answer is obvious. It is their perfect good faith itself, and their consequent veneration for what they look on as sacred and specially blessed of God, and not any fear or doubt, that would make them rise in indignation against what, in their eyes, would be a profane and unwarrantable desecration.

There are limits, they would protest, to the intrusive and irreverent meddling of men under pretexts of science. Are there not many points in pathology and physiology on which further knowledge is very desirable—a knowledge which some think can be reached best and most surely, if not only, by vivisection, especially of human subjects, whether in normal health or presenting peculiar developments? Shall we, therefore, in the interests of science, pick out such cases in a community, and deliver them over to be cut up alive, and their still living bodies to be explored by these science-seeking experimenters? Knowledge is good and profitable, undoubtedly; but human life is sacred, and must be preserved intact, even though these men remain in the dark on various obscure points.

So, too, holding as they do that the ampulla contains a portion of the veritable blood of St. Januarius, preserved by miracle of divine Providence, and miraculously liquefied on his feasts, the Neapolitans would shrink in horror from the sacrilegious profanity of delivering it over to the retorts and crucibles, and mortars and solutions, of a chemical laboratory.

Chemical experiments, they would say, are very respectable and very admirable in their place; but there are things too precious and too sacred to be submitted to them. In refusing to do so, the Neapolitans do not confess a sense of the weakness of their own cause. They rather manifest their sincere veneration for what they believe God has specially honored.

As for the plea that this test would solve the question, the Neapolitans would reply that for some minds nothing is ever solved. If men wish really to know the truth, let them examine the evidences which were appealed to before modern chemistry was invented. Those evidences still exist, and are ample and irrefragable. "They have Moses and the prophets; if they will not hear them, neither will they believe, though one rose from the dead."

One other objection remains: does God act uselessly? And of what possible use is this miracle? What is the benefit of wonderfully preserving from utter destruction, through so many centuries, a small portion of blood, and of causing it to soften or liquefy fifteen or twenty times a year, when brought, even if reverently, close to the head of the martyr from whose veins it flowed? What good does this do? Is it not so trifling and insignificant a thing as to be almost ridiculous, and entirely unworthy of the majesty of God?

Who shall presume to say that it is unworthy of God—of that God without whose knowledge and permission not a hair can fall from our heads—of that Saviour who mixed clay with the spittle of his mouth, and therewith touched the eyes of the blind man, that sight might be restored to them? It is not for us to decide what is becoming or unbecoming for God to do.

Who shall say that it is useless? Has not the faith of a simple-minded people been confirmed and strengthened by it, to such a degree that the truths of divine revelation and the obligations of man before God are to them verities as strong, as clear, and as real in their daily life as is the sunlight that beams down on their fair land? How many sinners have been led, through it, to repentance and amendment of life? How often have the indifferent been stirred up to avoid evil and to do good, and the good animated to greater fervor and earnestness in deeds of piety and virtue? And, after all, are not these the grand purposes of all God's dealings with men?

Nor is this miracle—for such we call it, although the church has never spoken authoritatively on the point— alien from doctrine. Wrought in honor of a sainted and martyred bishop, it is a perpetual testimony to the truth of the doctrines he preached, and of the church which glories in him as one of her exemplary and venerated ministers; it is a confirmation of the homage and veneration she pays to him because he chose rather to sacrifice his life than to deny the Saviour who had redeemed and illumined him. Wrought within her fold, it is a permanent evidence that she is in fact and in spirit the same now as in the early days of persecution—the ever true and faithful church of Christ.

It is a confirmation, likewise, of the doctrine of the resurrection of the dead — that special doctrine which the apostles put forth so prominently in the beginning of their preaching; which was ever present to the minds of the early Christians, cheering and strengthening them when this world was dark around them; which formed the frequent theme of their pastoral instructions and their mutual exhortations, and became the prevailing subject of their household and their sacred ornamentation in their homes and in their oratories, and over their tombs in the catacombs; which gave a special tone to their faith, their hope, and their charity and love of God, and was, as it were, the very life-blood of their Christianity.

Nowadays, outside the church, how faint, comparatively, has belief in this doctrine become, or, rather,

has it not died out almost completely from the thoughts and the hearts of men? Within the church, the solemn rites of Christian sepulture, burying the dead in consecrated ground, tells us of it. The preservation and the veneration of the relics of saints and martyrs teach it still more strongly. Does not tangible evidence, as it were, come to it anew from heaven by this constant and perpetual miracle, showing that the bodies of the sainted dead are in the custody of him who made them, and who has promised that he will raise them up again in glory?

Finally, this miracle seems to us especially adapted to our own age, when over-much knowledge is making men mad. Men are so lifted up by their progress, especially in natural sciences, that they have come to feel that they can dispense with God and substitute NATURE in his stead, with her multifarious and unchangeable laws. They boast that, under the light of their newly-acquired knowledge, everything is already, or will soon be, susceptible of natural explanation. As for miracles—direct interventions of God in the affairs of the world, reversing or suspending, in special cases, these ordinary laws of nature—they scout the idea. All past accounts of miracles, no matter when or by whom recorded, they hold to be either accounts of natural events warped and distorted by excited and unrestrained imaginations, or else the pure fictions of superstition and credulity. They are sure that, in the first case, had there been present witnesses of sufficient knowledge and caution—such knowledge and caution as they possess—the accounts of those events would have come down to us in a far simpler garb, and unclothed with this miraculous robing. They are equally sure that, in the other case, education, especially in the physical sciences, would have forbidden the creation of those numberless fictions.

Well, here, in the light of this nineteenth century, in one of the most polished, most delightful, and most accessible cities of Italy—centuries ago the largest, and even now the fourth largest, in Europe—there occurs an event to which their attention is invited. It is not an event of which a few only can be witnesses, and which all others must learn on their testimony. It occurs in public. It occurs fifteen or twenty times each year, and year after year. All may scrutinize it again and again, as often and as closely as they please. No mystery is made of anything about it. We admit it has come down to us from the middle ages, dark, ignorant, and superstitious as they are alleged to have been. But then, if it belongs to the past, it occurs still, and belongs equally to this nineteenth century. Moreover, it comes directly in contact with those physical sciences in which they think themselves strongest, and it should, therefore, interest them, and claim their attention.

Will they accept the invitation? We think very few will heed it.

Many would not dare to believe in a miracle nowadays, not even if it happened to themselves. They take their ground beforehand. Since miracles are impossible, any special one must of necessity be false—either a fraud or a delusion. They know from the beginning what the result of inquiring into this one must be—why give themselves unnecessary trouble? Such minds choose their own side, and implicitly choose the consequences that follow.

Others pretend to examine, but do it with a resolute and unshakable predetermination that this must *not* be found out to be a miracle. They foster a prejudice which may blind their eyes to the light; and they, too, make themselves equally responsible for their conclusion and its consequences.

But if any one—Catholic, Protestant, or Rationalist—will examine it seriously and candidly, no matter how closely and patiently—nay, the more closely and patiently, the more surely—he will come to the same inevitable conclusion to which such an examination has heretofore led so many other candid and intelligent inquirers: *Digitus Dei est hic:* The Finger of God is here.

www.ingramcontent.com/pod-product-compliance
Lightning Source LLC
Chambersburg PA
CBHW020327090426
42735CB00009B/1436